T0266764

An Analysis of

Yasser Tabbaa's

The Transformation of Islamic Art During the Sunni Revival

Bilal Badat

Published by Macat International Ltd
24:13 Coda Centre, 189 Munster Road, London SW6 6AW.

Distributed exclusively by Routledge
2 Park Square, Milton Park, Abingdon, Oxon OX14 4RN
711 Third Avenue, New York, NY 10017, USA

Routledge is an imprint of the Taylor & Francis Group, an informa business

www.macat.com
info@macat.com

Cataloguing in Publication Data
A catalogue record for this book is available from the British Library.
Library of Congress Cataloguing-in-Publication Data is available upon request.
Cover illustration: Pablo Casado

ISBN 978-1-912303-96-0 (hardback)
ISBN 978-1-912284-67-2 (paperback)
ISBN 978-1-912284-81-8 (e-book)

Notice
The information in this book is designed to orientate readers of the work under analysis,
to elucidate and contextualise its key ideas and themes, and to aid in the development
of critical thinking skills. It is not meant to be used, nor should it be used, as a
substitute for original thinking or in place of original writing or research. References and
notes are provided for informational purposes and their presence does not constitute
endorsement of the information or opinions therein. This book is presented solely for
educational purposes. It is sold on the understanding that the publisher is not engaged
to provide any scholarly advice. The publisher has made every effort to ensure that
this book is accurate and up-to-date, but makes no warranties or representations with
regard to the completeness or reliability of the information it contains. The information
and the opinions provided herein are not guaranteed or warranted to produce particular
results and may not be suitable for students of every ability. The publisher shall not be
liable for any loss, damage or disruption arising from any errors or omissions, or from
the use of this book, including, but not limited to, special, incidental, consequential or
other damages caused, or alleged to have been caused, directly or indirectly, by the
information contained within.

CONTENTS

THE MACAT LIBRARY

The Macat Library is a series of unique academic explorations of seminal works in the humanities and social sciences – books and papers that have had a significant and widely recognised impact on their disciplines. It has been created to serve as much more than just a summary of what lies between the covers of a great book. It illuminates and explores the influences on, ideas of, and impact of that book. Our goal is to offer a learning resource that encourages critical thinking and fosters a better, deeper understanding of important ideas.

Each publication is divided into three Sections: Influences, Ideas, and Impact. Each Section has four Modules. These explore every important facet of the work, and the responses to it.

This Section-Module structure makes a Macat Library book easy to use, but it has another important feature. Because each Macat book is written to the same format, it is possible (and encouraged!) to cross-reference multiple Macat books along the same lines of inquiry or research. This allows the reader to open up interesting interdisciplinary pathways.

To further aid your reading, lists of glossary terms and people mentioned are included at the end of this book (these are indicated by an asterisk [*] throughout) – as well as a list of works cited.

Macat has worked with the University of Cambridge to identify the elements of critical thinking and understand the ways in which six different skills combine to enable effective thinking. Three allow us to fully understand a problem; three more give us the tools to solve it. Together, these six skills make up the **PACIER** model of critical thinking. They are:

ANALYSIS – understanding how an argument is built
EVALUATION – exploring the strengths and weaknesses of an argument
INTERPRETATION – understanding issues of meaning

CREATIVE THINKING – coming up with new ideas and fresh connections
PROBLEM-SOLVING – producing strong solutions
REASONING – creating strong arguments

To find out more, visit **WWW.MACAT.COM.**

CRITICAL THINKING AND *THE TRANSFORMATION OF ISLAMIC ART DURING THE SUNNI REVIVAL*

Primary critical thinking skill: INTERPRETATION
Secondary critical thinking skill: CREATIVE THINKING

Yasser Tabbaa is classic example of an interpretive and creative thinker. In *The Transformation of Islamic Art During the Sunni Revival*, Tabbaa is careful to clarify meaning in his descriptions of the characteristic forms of medieval Islamic art such as calligraphy, arabesque, and *muqarnas* – all of which he sees as symbolically charged icons of the Sunni revival. According to Tabbaa, these forms embodied and expressed specific political and theological messages intended to bolster the political authority of the Abbasids and promulgate traditionalist Sunni theology. This innovative hypothesis distinguishes *The Transformation of Islamic Art* from the majority of studies on medieval Islamic art, which either limit, ignore, or completely reject the larger issues of historical or contextual meaning.

In order to substantiate his argument, Tabbaa constructs a new historical and cultural framework in which to set the profound transformations in Islamic art and architectural during the medieval period, examining both the political and theological dimensions of the Sunni revival as well as contemporaneous developments in calligraphic and ornamental forms. In doing so, Tabbaa is able to demonstrate with exemplary lucidity how transformations in medieval Islamic art and architecture reflected and embodied parallel changes in politics and piety.

ABOUT THE AUTHOR OF THE ORIGINAL WORK

Dr. Yasser Tabbaa has taught and published widely in the field of Islamic art and architecture for over 30 years. Working at the intersection of politics, social history, religion, and aesthetics, Tabbaa established his reputation as a highly original and critical thinker with the 2001 publication of *The Transformation of Islamic Art During the Sunni Revival.* In addition to writing books and articles, Tabbaa has also taught Islamic art and architecture at universities across the US and the Middle East, including the Massachusetts Institute of Technology (MIT), the University of Michigan, Oberlin College, and New York University, Abu Dhabi.

ABOUT THE AUTHOR OF THE ANALYSIS

Dr. Bilal Badat teaches Islamic art and architecture at the University of Tübingen, Germany. Badat wrote his PhD on pedagogy in Ottoman calligraphy at the Prince's School of Traditional Arts, London, and undertook a traditional apprenticeship in Islamic calligraphy as part of his research. Badat also worked as specialist curator of Islamic art at the British Museum. Much of his current work focuses on Ottoman art and architecture, the transmission of calligraphic knowledge over time, and the master-student relationship in Islamic calligraphy.

ABOUT MACAT

GREAT WORKS FOR CRITICAL THINKING

Macat is focused on making the ideas of the world's great thinkers accessible and comprehensible to everybody, everywhere, in ways that promote the development of enhanced critical thinking skills.

It works with leading academics from the world's top universities to produce new analyses that focus on the ideas and the impact of the most influential works ever written across a wide variety of academic disciplines. Each of the works that sit at the heart of its growing library is an enduring example of great thinking. But by setting them in context – and looking at the influences that shaped their authors, as well as the responses they provoked – Macat encourages readers to look at these classics and game-changers with fresh eyes. Readers learn to think, engage and challenge their ideas, rather than simply accepting them.

'Macat offers an amazing first-of-its-kind tool for
interdisciplinary learning and research. Its focus on works
that transformed their disciplines and its rigorous approach,
drawing on the world's leading experts and educational institutions,
opens up a world-class education to anyone.'

Andreas Schleicher
Director for Education and Skills, Organisation for Economic
Co-operation and Development

'Macat is taking on some of the major challenges in university
education … They have drawn together a strong team of active
academics who are producing teaching materials that are
novel in the breadth of their approach.'

Prof Lord Broers,
former Vice-Chancellor of the University of Cambridge

'The Macat vision is exceptionally exciting. It focuses
upon new modes of learning which analyse and explain seminal texts
which have profoundly influenced world thinking and so social and
economic development. It promotes the kind of critical thinking
which is essential for any society and economy.
This is the learning of the future.'

Rt Hon Charles Clarke, former UK Secretary of State for Education

'The Macat analyses provide immediate access to the critical
conversation surrounding the books that have shaped their
respective discipline, which will make them an invaluable resource
to all of those, students and teachers, working in the field.'

Professor William Tronzo, University of California at San Diego

WAYS IN TO THE TEXT

KEY POINTS

- Yasser Tabbaa is a historian of Islamic art and architecture who has made major contributions to the study of the art and architecture of the Islamic world during the medieval period.

- *The Transformation of Islamic Art During the Sunni Revival* explores how the political, theological, and cultural changes that occurred during the Sunni revival contributed to the development of Islamic art and architecture.

- *The Transformation of Islamic Art* has a broad appeal for scholars and students in fields of Islamic art, history, and theology.

Who Is Yasser Tabbaa?

Yasser Tabbaa has taught and published widely in the field of Islamic art and architecture for over 30 years. Working at the intersection of politics, social history, religion, and aesthetics, Tabbaa has written numerous books and articles on a wide variety of subjects including Islamic art and architecture, Islamic gardens, poetics, Islamic ornament, and Islamic calligraphy. Tabbaa has also taught Islamic art and architecture at universities across the US and the Middle East, including at the Massachusetts Institute of Technology (MIT), the University of Michigan, Oberlin College, and New York University, Abu Dhabi.

Tabbaa obtained his PhD in 1983 from New York University, where he studied under the tutelage of Richard Ettinghausen,* one of the founding fathers of the discipline of Islamic art history in the United States. After Ettinghausen's death in 1980, Tabbaa continued his PhD under the supervision of the archaeologist and art historian of Islamic art and architecture Oleg Grabar* and Professor in the history of Islamic art Priscilla Soucek.*[1] Following the completion of his thesis, entitled "The Architectural Patronage of Nūr al-Dīn* 1146–74," Tabbaa went on to chart a highly successful career as an academic, publishing a significant number of articles and book chapters on the art and architecture of Syria and the Jazira* during the medieval period. Tabbaa also published three books on Islamic art and architecture, entitled *Constructions of Power and Piety in Medieval Aleppo* (1997), *The Transformation of Islamic Art During the Sunni Revival* (2001), and *Najaf: History and Heritage* (2014). Tabbaa is currently working on a fourth book, which carries the preliminary title *In the Presence of the Imam: Architecture, Ritual, and Representation in Shi'i Shrine Architecture.*

What Does *The Transformation Of Islamic Art* Say?

The Transformation of Islamic Art During the Sunni Revival, Tabbaa explains, "discusses the transformation undergone by Islamic architecture and ornament during the medieval period and investigates the cultural processes by which meaning was produced within the resulting new forms."[2] On a more fundamental level, Tabbaa argues that the Sunni* revival, defined as the political and theological movement which sought to reaffirm traditionalist* Sunni Islam and unite Sunni dynasties under the political umbrella of the Abbasid* caliphate,* inspired the transformation of key elements of Islamic art and architecture, including proportional calligraphy, public inscriptions, vegetal and geometric arabesque,* and *muqarnas** vaulting in Iran, Iraq, and Syria during the eleventh and twelfth centuries.

Tabbaa proposes that the transformation of these artistic and architectural devices and their subsequent dissemination took place within a highly confrontational atmosphere marked by political and theological rivalry between the traditionalist Sunni Abbasids, Seljuqs,* and post-Seljuq dynasties on one side, against their main opponents, the Fatimid* Ismailis* in Egypt. As Tabbaa argues, in order to reassert their waning political and religious authority, the Abbasids created and systematized new artistic and architectural devices in the Abbasid capital, Baghdad, to serve as visual signs of a Sunni revival under the Abbasid caliphate. These newly created forms embodied and expressed the theological tenets of traditionalist Sunni theology and functioned as symbols of Abbasid political authority.

The Abbasids then actively sponsored the dissemination of these newly created forms throughout the Islamic world, where they were adopted, developed, and further disseminated by a succession of Sunni dynasties such as the Ghaznavids,* Seljuqs, Zangids,* and Ayyubids.* By adopting and developing the forms created by the Abbasids, these Sunni dynasties could demonstrate their allegiance to the Abbasids (which bolstered the temporal and spiritual authority of the Abbasids) and at the same secure a legitimate political and religious status of their own through recognition and appointment from the Abbasid caliphate.

Tabbaa argues that the mutual benefits of this political and artistic alignment accelerated the spread of the newly created forms across the Islamic world and projected an image of Sunni unity. Furthermore, this structure of reciprocating gestures between the Abbasids and other Sunni polities articulated a strong visual distinction between the traditionalist Sunnis and their main adversaries, the Ismaili Fatimids of Egypt.

Thus, Tabbaa interprets medieval Islamic art and architecture as a necessary expression and application of Islamic theological and political dogma endured during a time of intense conflict and sectarianism.* This interpretative approach distinguishes Tabbaa from earlier scholars of Islamic art, who predominantly focused on describing and classifying visual forms and rarely subjected the meaning of those forms to historical scrutiny.[3] In this regard, *The Transformation of Islamic Art* stands as a thought-provoking alternative to positivist* studies of Islamic art and architecture and stimulates a healthy debate for the field as a whole.

Why Does *The Transformation Of Islamic Art* Matter?

One of the primary reasons why *The Transformation of Islamic Art* matters is that it stands as an effective working model for how to subject transformations in art to historical scrutiny. Tabbaa begins his book by outlining the political, religious, and cultural changes that occurred in the early medieval Islamic world, then proceeds to explain how these changes shaped contemporaneous developments in Islamic art and architecture. Through this contextual approach, Tabbaa is able to bridge the gap between historical speculation and applied artistry and effectively demonstrate how architecture and the visual arts can be expressions of political and religious dogma as well as a reflection of political, cultural, and religious identity.

The Transformation of Islamic Art is also significant for its essential thesis, which argues that new identities and concepts are created through challenge and controversy. This thesis runs counter to essentialist* and positivist approaches to Islamic art, which emphasize the overriding unity of Islamic art and seemingly ignore the apparent changes and differing meanings attributed to Islamic art over time. By focusing on ruptures rather than continuities, therefore, *The Transformation of Islamic Art* stands as an exemplar for students seeking to rationalize change and artistic development against the dynamic forces of conflict and political upheaval.

A third reason why *The Transformation of Islamic Art* is important is its value as a source for students seeking to understand the historical contours of the early medieval Islamic world. *The Transformation of Islamic Art* collates a host of important material from a wide range of diverse sources to explain an array of issues and controversies, including the challenges faced by the Abbasid caliphate during the tenth through twelfth centuries; the theological tenets and conflicts that developed during this period; the emergence of powerful regional dynasties such as the Ghaznavids, Zangids, Seljuqs, and Ayyubids; the establishment of the Fatimid counter-caliphate in Egypt in 969; and the dawn of the Crusades.* As such, a reading of *The Transformation of Islamic* Art has a broad appeal to those interested in understanding the origins and nature of sectarian conflicts and political formations in the Islamic world and also for those seeking an entry into the disciplines of Islamic history, Islamic theology, and Islamic art and architecture.

To date, the *Transformation of Islamic Art* has been cited over 70 times in scholarly publications, and Tabbaa's work continues to influence, inform, and inspire the research methods of historians of Islamic art and architecture.

NOTES

1   Yasser Tabbaa, "Invented Pieties: The Rediscovery and Rebuilding of the Shrine of Sayyida Ruqayya in Damascus, 1975-2006," *Artibus Asiae*, 67, No. 1, Pearls from Water. Rubies from Stone. Studies in Islamic Art in Honor of Priscilla Soucek, Part II (2007), 95.

2   Yasser Tabbaa, *The Transformation of Islamic Art During the Sunni Revival*, (London: I.B. Tauris & Co., Ltd. 2001), 3.

3   Tabbaa, *Transformation*, 6.

SECTION 1
INFLUENCES

MODULE 1
THE AUTHOR AND THE HISTORICAL CONTEXT

KEY POINTS

- *The Transformation of Islamic Art During the Sunni Revival* is the first book to investigate the impact of the theological tenets of the Sunni revival on contemporaneous transformations in calligraphic, ornamental, and architectural forms across the medieval Islamic world.

- Tabbaa has taught and published widely in the field of Islamic art and architecture for over 30 years.

- Three pioneers in the field of Islamic art and architecture supervised Tabbaa's doctoral thesis: Richard Ettinghausen, Oleg Grabar, and Priscilla Soucek.

Why Read This Text?

Yasser Tabbaa's *The Transformation of Islamic Art During the Sunni Revival* is the first book to investigate the impact of the theological tenets of the Sunni revival on contemporaneous transformations in calligraphic, ornamental, and architectural forms across the medieval Islamic world. As Tabbaa explains, the development of these forms and their subsequent dissemination took place within a highly confrontational atmosphere marked by political and theological rivalry between the traditionalist Sunni Abbasids and their main opponents, the Ismaili Fatimids of Egypt. Tabbaa argues that the Abbasids created and systematized artistic forms such as calligraphy, arabesque, and *muqarnas* to function as visual signs of the Sunni revival, thus facilitating the re-emergence of the Abbasid caliphate in a more orthodox image. The subsequent spread of these artistic forms from Baghdad throughout

> ❝ By problematizing instead of glossing over the innovations, ruptures, and discontinuities, that characterized the Islamic world of the eleventh and twelfth centuries, this book strives for a better understanding of the mechanisms of change and the production of meaning in Islamic art and architecture. ❞
>
> Yasser Tabbaa, *The Transformation of Islamic Art During the Sunni Revival*

the Islamic world was actively sponsored by the Abbasids and further disseminated by Seljuq and post-Seljuq proponents of the traditionalist Sunni revival. This dissemination projected an image of unity between Sunni polities and articulated a strong visual distinction between the Sunnis and the Ismaili Fatimids.

Through its investigation of change and controversy, *The Transformation of Islamic Art* challenges the positivist and ethno-nationalist* approaches that still permeate the study of Islamic art, going beyond the purely descriptive and essentializing narratives of these works to offer a thought-provoking explanation for the profound cultural changes that transpired in the medieval Islamic world. The importance of this book also lies in its collation of a diverse array of critical material, including textual sources, archaeological evidence, and existing works of art and architecture across the Islamic world. In both its subject matter and approach, *The Transformation of Islamic Art* makes original contributions to the field of Islamic art and architecture and engenders a lively debate about the meanings that artistic forms acquired in the Islamic world and how new concepts and identities can be created through intense periods of rupture and change.

Author's Life

Tabbaa has taught and published widely in the field of Islamic art and architecture for over 30 years. Working at the intersection of politics, social history, religion, and aesthetics, Tabbaa has written numerous books and articles on a wide variety of subjects including Islamic art and architecture, Islamic gardens, poetics, Islamic ornament, and Islamic calligraphy. Tabbaa has also taught Islamic art and architecture at universities across the United States and the Middle East, including at the Massachusetts Institute of Technology (MIT), the University of Memphis, Southern Methodist University, the University of Michigan, Oberlin College, and New York University, Abu Dhabi.

Tabbaa obtained his PhD in 1983 from New York University. His thesis, entitled "The Architectural Patronage of Nūr al-Dīn 1146-74," was completed under the supervision of Priscilla Soucek and two pioneers in the field of Islamic art and architecture, Richard Ettinghausen and Oleg Grabar, both distinguished scholars who played a significant role in developing and defining the field as it stands today. After completing his thesis, Tabbaa went on to establish his reputation as a specialist in the art and architecture of medieval Syria and the Jazira with the publication of numerous articles and books on the subject. Tabbaa is currently working on a fourth book, which carries the preliminary title *In the Presence of the Imam: Architecture, Ritual, and Representation in Shi'i Shrine Architecture.*

Author's Background

The global events that followed the remarkable rise of the oil-producing countries of the Middle East stimulated an unprecedented level of academic interest in the region. In the United States, this increased interest was hallmarked by the opening of new Islamic galleries at the Metropolitan Museum of Art (October 1975), which Ettinghausen curated. The increased interest in the Middle East was also marked by the creation of the Aga Khan Program for Islamic Architecture at Harvard and MIT in 1979, led by Grabar.[1] Both Ettinghausen and Grabar would go on to have a monumental impact on the field of Islamic art and architecture, advancing scholarship through a numerous lectures, curated exhibitions, and the publication of articles and books, including Grabar's seminal work *The Formation of Islamic Art* and Ettinghausen's *Arab Painting*. Both Ettinghausen and Grabar helped shape Tabbaa's academic career; both scholars supervised Tabbaa's doctoral thesis at New York, and Grabar provided valuable scholarly insights on *The Transformation of Islamic Art* from its incipient form as a dissertation to its final arrangement as a book.[2]

The 1970s and the following decades also witnessed a series of tumultuous events and conflicts across the Middle East, starting with the Iranian revolution of 1979* and continuing with the Soviet invasion of Afghanistan,* the Iran-Iraq war,* the Gulf War,* the US led invasion of Afghanistan and Iraq,* and the Syrian Civil War.* Although it may be sheer coincidence, it is hard to imagine that the number and severity of these conflicts in the late 1980s and 1990s did not influence Tabbaa as he was researching and writing *The Transformation of Islamic Art*, a text that explores a similarly charged atmosphere of rivalry, rupture, and confrontation across the Islamic world. Fortunately, Tabbaa was able to document buildings in Syria prior to the civil war, and he was also able to travel throughout Iraq in the 1980s despite ongoing difficulties in the region.[3] As Tabbaa mentions in his preface, this freedom of travel was thanks in large measure to the assistance of Issa Sulaiman* and Muayyad Basim Demerji,* successive Directors General of Antiquities in Iraq.[4]

NOTES

1   Sheila S. Blair and Jonathan M. Bloom, "The Mirage of Islamic Art: Reflections on the Study of an Unwieldy Field," *The Art Bulletin*, 85, 1 (2003): 156-57.

2   Yasser Tabbaa, "Invented Pieties: The Rediscovery and Rebuilding of the
     Shrine of Sayyida Ruqayya in Damascus, 1975-2006," *Artibus Asiae*, 67,
     No. 1, Pearls from Water. Rubies from Stone. Studies in Islamic Art in Honor
     of Priscilla Soucek, Part II (2007), 95; Yasser Tabbaa, *The Transformation of
     Islamic Art during the Sunni Revival*, (London: I.B. Tauris & Co., Ltd. 2001),
     XII.

3   Tabbaa, *Transformation*, XII.

4   Tabbaa, *Transformation*, XII.

MODULE 2
ACADEMIC CONTEXT

KEY POINTS

- The field of Islamic art and architecture encompasses a diversity of approaches to the study of visual material.
- Oleg Grabar's *The Formation of Islamic Art* and Gülrü Necipoğlu's *The Topkapı Scroll* were major influences on *The Transformation of Islamic Art*.
- Much like Grabar and Necipoğlu, Tabbaa adopts a historical and culturally specific approach to the study of Islamic art and architecture.

The Work In Its Context

Yasser Tabbaa's *The Transformation of Islamic Art During the Sunni Revival* emerges from the field of Islamic art and architecture. In broad terms, this field encompasses the study of the art and architecture produced over fourteen centuries in Islamic lands. These lands are typically defined as the geographies where Islam spread and flourished following the initial Muslim conquests in the seventh and eighth centuries and includes regions with significant Muslim populations, such as tropical Africa, Eastern Europe, and Western China.

In terms of chronology and typology, the scope of Islamic art and architecture encompasses nearly all forms of art and architecture produced from the birth of Islam in the seventh century through the dissolution of the Ottoman and Mughal dynasties in the early twentieth century, including everything from monumental congregational mosques patronized by sultans to household pottery produced by anonymous craftsmen in local kilns. In this regard, the

❝ Since I first contemplated writing this book, two extremely important works have filled the very gap I have attempted to illustrate ... These two books, by [Oleg] Grabar and [Gülrü] Necipoğlu, revisit long-untrodden grounds and cast a fresh look at issues long ignored by serious art historians. ❞

Yasser Tabbaa, *The Transformation of Islamic Art During the Sunni Revival*

term "Islamic art" is not comparable to other denominations such as "Christian" or "Hindu" art, which typically refer to sacred art used for ritualistic purposes in specifically religious settings. As the historian of Islamic art Sheila Blair* observes:

The term "Islamic art" seems to be a convenient misnomer for everything left over from everywhere else. It is most easily defined by what it is not: neither a region, nor a period, nor a school, nor a movement, nor a dynasty, but the visual culture of a place and time when the people (or at least their leaders) espoused a particular religion.[1]

This rather broad definition of Islamic art emerged out of nineteenth century Orientalist* scholarship which grouped together the diversity of Islamic artistic and architectural traditions under the universal and common conception of "Islamic art" or "Islamic culture."[2] In doing so, Orientalist scholarship overlooked the cultural complexity of Islamic lands and ignored the historical specificity of individual monuments and objects. Another great failure of the Orientalist project was to essentialize the nature of Islamic art as reflection of universal themes such as the transcendent nature of the word of God or the spirit of Islamic revelation, regardless of the temporal or geographical contexts of the objects of study.[3] This problematic perspective then gave way to the equally problematic ethno-national categorization of Islamic art as a monolithic entity expressed through a hierarchy of Arab, Persian, Turkish, or Indian national character traits.[4]

However, since that time, scholarship on Islamic art has moved on. Following the pioneering efforts of Grabar in the early 1970s, historians of Islamic art have developed a diversity of approaches to studying and writing about Islamic art and architecture and have utilized a variety of methodologies to deconstruct the universalizing approaches of early Orientalist scholars.

Overview Of The Field

In an attempt to establish an intellectual context for *The Transformation of Islamic Art*, Tabbaa acknowledges two key works. The first of these is Grabar's highly influential book, *The Formation of Islamic Art*. First published in 1972, *The Formation of Islamic Art* focuses on how Islamic art and architecture developed out of the historical and aesthetic heritage of late antiquity.* Ultimately, Grabar argues that early Muslim communities formulated a new and recognizably distinct Islamic visual tradition by first developing new artistic and architectural forms to correspond to the specific needs of Islamic society, and second by appropriating and recombining the existing styles, motifs, and forms of newly conquered lands to cater to the political, princely, and pietistic requirements of the nascent Muslim community. Through this creative process, early Muslims were able to establish a uniquely Islamic language of art and architecture.

Grabar delivers his thesis by contextualizing early Islamic art and architecture against the historical backdrop of early Islamic ritualistic, cultural, and political practices. By adopting this historical-contextual approach, Grabar goes beyond the formal and classificatory descriptions of late nineteenth and early twentieth century scholars to offer a thoughtful analysis of how Islamic art and architecture reflected broader political, religious, and cultural motives. Furthermore, and perhaps crucially for Tabbaa, by developing an intellectual framework for the study of Islamic art and architecture, Grabar establishes a working model for how to give meaning to a body of visual material.

The second key work is Gülrü Necipoğlu's* *The Topkapi Scroll*. Necipoğlu offers an in-depth discussion of the content and broader intellectual context of the late fifteenth- century Topkapi Scroll, a compendium of architectural drawings used for the generation of two- and three-dimensional patterns on walls and in vaults. He argues that the geometrical *girih** mode, a style of geometry characterized by the use of interlaced straps and star patterns, evolved out of the popularization of theoretical mathematics, optics, and geometry in late-Abbasid Baghdad. Furthermore, Necipoğlu proposes that the *girih* mode was identified as an ideological visual symbol of the early-medieval Sunni revival in the eastern Islamic world. Much like Grabar, therefore, Necipoğlu rejects the positivist and essentialist approaches to Islamic art that dominated the field from the late-nineteenth century, replacing them with historical, theological, and semiotic modes of interpretation. She explores the sources of the aesthetic and cultural principles that shaped Islamic art and provides an insight into the ways in which Islamic visual languages could express aesthetic theories and political identities.

Academic Influences

In the preface and introduction to *The Transformation of Islamic Art*, Tabbaa cites both *The Formation of Islamic Art* and *The Topkapi Scroll* as influences on his work.[5] Much like his former mentor Grabar, Tabbaa adopts a historical and culturally specific approach to the study of Islamic art and architecture. In fact, Tabbaa says the *Formation of Islamic Art* influenced his thinking at an early stage in his academic career:

Reading *Formation* was especially significant for me, for it led me to think of questions of social history and patronage for my dissertation on Nūr al-Dīn … *Formation* remains his most important book, marking as it does a decisive shift in the field from product to process and from focusing on the object to examining its contextual relations.[6]

In terms of scope, Tabbaa states that *The Transformation of Islamic Art* seeks to demonstrate the expansion of knowledge in the field of Islamic art since *The Formation of Islamic Art*. Furthermore, Tabbaa focuses on the formal changes in Islamic art in the middle rather than the early period that formed the focus of Grabar's work.[7]

Tabbaa also acknowledges a debt to Necipoğlu's *Topkapi Scroll*.[8] Tabbaa praised Necipoğlu's contextual approach to the visual material, where she juxtaposes developments in Islamic ornament against theological and political discourses.[9] Tabbaa also agrees with Necipoğlu's conclusions that the full development of the *girih* mode "represented a new visual order projecting a shared ethos of unification around the religious authority of the Abbasid caliphate" and that the *girih* mode was connected to the theological tenets of the Sunni revival.[10] However, while Tabbaa fully accepts the interpretive parameters of Necipoğlu, he also seeks to provide a more specific timeframe for his work by focusing on the Sunni revival.[11] Tabbaa also departs from both Grabar and Necipoğlu by examining transformations in architecture and calligraphy during a specific moment of political and sectarian conflict.[12]

NOTES

1   Sheila S. Blair and Jonathan M. Bloom, "The Mirage of Islamic Art: Reflections on the Study of an Unwieldy Field," *The Art Bulletin*, 85, 1 (2003): 153.

2   Gülru Necipoğlu, "The Concept of Islamic Art: Inherited Discourses and New Approaches," in *Islamic Art and the Museum*, ed. Benoît Junod et al. (London, Saqi Books, 2012), 4.

3   Yasser Tabbaa, *The Transformation of Islamic Art During the Sunni Revival*, (London: I.B. Tauris & Co., Ltd. 2001), 4-5.

4   Necipoğlu, "The Concept of Islamic Art," 4.

5   Tabbaa, *Transformation*, 6.

6   Robert Hillenbrand, "Oleg Grabar: The Scholarly Legacy," *Journal of Art Historiography* 6 (June 2012): 24, fn 110, accessed August 18, 2017, https://arthistoriography.files.wordpress.com/2012/05/hillenbrand.pdf.

7   Tabbaa, *Transformation*, 6-7.

8   Tabbaa, *Transformation*, 6.

9   Tabbaa, *Transformation*, 76.

10   Tabbaa, *Transformation*, 77.

11   Tabbaa, *Transformation*, 77.

12   Tabbaa, *Transformation*, 6.

MODULE 3
THE PROBLEM

KEY POINTS

- *The Transformation of Islamic Art During the Sunni Revival* responds to the question of meaning in Islamic art.
- Archaeologists, Orientalists, and art historians have adopted contrasting perspectives on the question of meaning in Islamic art.
- Yasser Tabbaa argues that new meanings were attributed to Islamic art and architecture during moments of profound political, theological, and cultural change.

Core Question

Yasser Tabbaa's *The Transformation of Islamic Art During the Sunni Revival* investigates the question of meaning in Islamic art. Ultimately this question is concerned with whether the characteristic forms of Islamic art and architecture, such as calligraphy and the arabesque, symbolized or communicated certain political or religious messages through their appearance, or were simply decorative devices intended for the viewer's aesthetic pleasure. In his introduction, Tabbaa articulates the objectives of his book by posing the following questions:

How and why did such characteristic forms of Islamic art as arabesque, both vegetal and geometric, *muqarnas* vaulting, public inscriptions, and even calligraphy develop? Are these forms meaningful or merely decorative? Are they immanent features of Islamic art with universal meaning, or were they produced under specific historical conditions for a particular purpose or message? Did these forms convey religious messages, embody political propaganda, establish social distinctions, or display technical virtuosity?[1]

> ❝ In short, the attempt to explain the unity and variety of Islamic art through a combination of pan-Islamic and national character traits, either exalting or disparaging the artistic sensibilities of particular peoples, constitutes two sides of the same Orientalist coin. ❞
>
> Gülrü Necipoğlu, "The Concept of Islamic Art: Inherited Discourses and New Approaches," *Islamic Art and the Museum*

Tabbaa is interested in exploring the historical processes that produced meaning in new forms of Islamic art and investigates whether artists used those forms to express specific political ideas or affiliations, religious dogmas, or spiritual truths. Furthermore, he is keen to examine whether the meanings attributed to Islamic art were the same across time and space or changed depending on historical context. Through this academic analysis, Tabbaa enters a historical debate on the question of meaning that has polarized scholars of Islamic art.

The Participants

As Tabbaa outlines in his introduction, archaeologists, Orientalists, and art historians have adopted contrasting perspectives on the question of meaning in Islamic art. Early archaeologists such as K.A.C. Creswell,* J. Michael Rogers,* and Michael Meinecke* generally rejected the possibility of meaning in Islamic art, subscribing to the widely held belief at the time that Islamic art and architecture was not an expression of Islamic dogma.[2] This principle was constructed upon the belief that Muslim artists and architects did not leave behind a significant body of texts and documents that dealt with questions of meaning. As a result, Creswell and others exhibited a disinclination to take up the question of meaning, preferring instead to focus on the classification and description of monuments.[3]

Orientalists and art historians of an earlier generation such as Mehmet Aga-Oglu* adopted a different position, interpreting the main features of Islamic art—such as calligraphy, arabesque, and geometry—as timeless reflections of a so-called "Oriental" or "Islamic" spirit.[4] Within the Orientalist discourse, diversity in Islamic art is either overlooked in favor of a universal conception of Islamic art, or ambiguously linked to innate religious, ethnic, or national character traits.[5] More recently, a group of scholars including Titus Burckhardt* and Seyyed Hossein Nasr* have adopted a more theoretical and symbolic approach to understanding Islamic art. Often referred to as the Perennialist School* or the traditionalists, this group of scholars argues that Islamic art was an embodiment of the concepts of Divine Oneness and Unity.*[6] Within this hermeneutical framework, Islamic art is conceptualized as the crystallization of "heavenly realities on earth."[7] The traditionalists thus establish an overarching universal and spiritual framework for understanding Islamic art, but do not assist the reader in understanding how Islamic art developed over time.

Tabbaa observes a clear similarity between the Orientalist and traditionalist approaches: both "adopt an essentialist perspective that sees the various cultural forms in Islam, including art, as timeless atavisms regardless of their actual temporal or geographical coordinates and their role in society."[8] Thus, in terms of meaning, the Orientalists, early art historians, and traditionalists see Islamic art as a reflection of timeless Islamic religious and cultural values and overlook the possibility that the meaning of Islamic art may have changed over time. Furthermore, they fail to explore whether other meanings—political, theological, or otherwise—are expressed through Islamic art throughout the centuries.

In contrast, art historians such as Grabar and Necipoğlu have adopted a more contextual approach to the question of meaning in Islamic art. Informed by both archaeological evidence and textual analysis, both scholars have argued that the meanings attributed to

Islamic art changed according to historical circumstance. Within this framework of interpretation, Islamic art was a dynamic medium that embodied political, theological, and aesthetic concerns and reflected the constantly shifting socio-historical and artistic processes of the Islamic world.[9]

The Contemporary Debate

In *The Transformation of Islamic Art*, Tabbaa consciously positions himself against the Orientalist art historians and traditionalists. *The Transformation of Islamic Art* seeks to examine how Islamic art and architecture changed in the medieval period and investigate how new meanings were produced during moments of profound political, theological, and cultural change. As such, Tabbaa vehemently rejects what he considers to be the "ahistorical flounderings" of the essentialist Orientalists and traditionalists that generally fail to consider how meaning in Islamic art and architecture was produced and how those meanings may have changed over time.[10]

In seeking to discover how new meanings were engendered during the Sunni revival, Tabbaa also departs from the positivist approaches of Creswell and other early archaeologists. However, Tabbaa concedes that their archaeological methods are useful for establishing a standard of research and for providing a check against the excesses of interpretation.[11]

Tabbaa gravitates towards the approaches adopted by Grabar and Necipoğlu. Like both scholars, he investigates the historical processes by which meaning was produced in new forms of Islamic art and architecture. In the introduction to the *Transformation of Islamic Art*, Tabbaa praises Grabar and Necipoğlu for rejecting the "polarities of positivism and essentialism" and for dealing with questions of meaning in Islamic art and architecture in historical terms.[12] However, despite this conscious association, Tabbaa also explains what makes *The Transformation of Islamic Art* different: namely, that his book focuses in particular on the pivotal period of the Sunni revival and examines how new meanings, both political and theological, were expressed through a variety of artistic and architectural devices including calligraphy, inscriptions, arabesque, geometry, and *muqarnas* vaulting.[13]

NOTES

1   Yasser Tabbaa, *The Transformation of Islamic Art during the Sunni Revival*, (London: I.B. Tauris & Co., Ltd. 2001), 3.

2   Tabbaa, *Transformation*, 4.

3   Tabbaa, *Transformation*, 4.

4   Tabbaa, *Transformation*, 4.

5   Gülru Necipoğlu, "The Concept of Islamic Art: Inherited Discourses and New Approaches," in *Islamic Art and the Museum*, ed. Benoît Junod et al. (London, Saqi Books, 2012), 4-5.

6   Tabbaa, *Transformation*, 5.

7   Titus Burckhardt, *The Art of Islam: Language and Meaning* (London: World of Islam Festival Trust, 1976), xvi.

8   Tabbaa, *Transformation*, 5.

9   Gülrü Necipoğlu, *The Topkapi Scroll – Geometry and Ornament in Islamic Architecture* (Santa Monica, CA: The Getty Center for the History of Art and the Humanities, 1995); Oleg Grabar, *The Formation of Islamic Art* (New Haven, CT: Yale University Press, 1973); Oleg Grabar, *The Mediation of Ornament* (Princeton, NJ: Princeton University Press, 1992).

10 Tabbaa, *Transformation*, 7.

11 Tabbaa, *Transformation*, 4.

12 Tabbaa, *Transformation*, 6

13 Tabbaa, *Transformation*, 6 and 77.

MODULE 4
THE AUTHOR'S CONTRIBUTION

KEY POINTS

- Yasser Tabbaa argues that specific religio-political, social, and technological forces shaped medieval Islamic art and architecture.

- The rivalries between the Sunni Seljuq-Zangids and the Ismaili Fatimids were played out over a number of arenas including politics, theology, propaganda, architecture, and visual culture.

- *The Transformation of Islamic Art During the Sunni Revival* is distinguished from other works by its more acute focus on the challenges and conflicts that characterized the Islamic world of the eleventh and twelfth centuries.

Author's Aims

Yasser Tabbaa's *The Transformation of Islamic Art During the Sunni Revival* is the first book to systematically explore the impact of political, religious, and cultural changes in the Islamic world on the development of Islamic art and architecture during the early medieval period. Tabbaa's explicit aim is to investigate whether the emergence of new forms of Islamic art during the eleventh and twelfth centuries in Iran, Iraq, and Syria was related to or inspired by profound shifts in the contemporaneous political and religious landscape of the Islamic world. Furthermore, Tabbaa seeks to explore the cultural processes by which meaning was attributed to these new forms and how these meanings may have varied across time and space.

Tabbaa's argument in this book is that that the new calligraphic and ornamental forms produced during the medieval period encapsulated and embodied the religious and political ideologies of

> 66 Art, like cultures and even religions, defines itself against its opponents, and the more intense the conflict, the sharper this self-image. 99
>
> Yasser Tabbaa, *The Transformation of Islamic Art During the Sunni Revival*

the Sunni revival, taking on specific meanings that reflected the controversies and conflicts of the medieval Islamic world.[1] Prior to this book, scholars of Islamic art had either dismissed the notion that Islamic art and architecture could be an expression of Islamic dogma, or argued that Islamic art reflected a timeless Islamic essence that permeated all forms.[2] By arguing that medieval Islamic art and architecture was shaped by specific religious, political, social, and technological forces, therefore, Tabbaa not only challenges the orthodox position held by earlier scholars, but also makes a highly original contribution to the field by demonstrating how meaning can be represented in new forms.

Approach

Tabbaa explores how new meanings were produced in Islamic art and architecture by focusing on how conflicts, challenges, and controversies contributed to the development of calligraphy, arabesque, and *muqarnas* vaulting. As he explains in the introduction to his book, the rivalries and divisions between the Sunni Seljuq-Zangids and the Ismaili Fatimids were especially virulent during the early medieval period and were played out over a number of arenas including politics, theology, and propaganda. Tabbaa argues: "It stands to reason, therefore, that it was also played out in architecture and visual culture and that its dynamic forces of conflict, change, and self-definition, not the prescripts of a static Islam, were behind the transformations in medieval Islamic architecture."[3]

Thus, Tabbaa's approach to answering the question of meaning is to examine how art is defined through moments of conflict, political upheaval, and sectarian schism. In Tabbaa's view, "Art, like cultures and even religions, defines itself against its opponents, and the more intense the conflict, the sharper this self-image."[4]

This approach to understanding the production of meaning in Islamic art distinguishes Tabbaa from earlier Orientalist, perennialist, and positivist scholars, who either overlooked or dismissed the possibility that Islamic art could be an expression of theological or political controversy. Instead, they argued that Islamic art developed smoothly within a predetermined set of religious prescriptions. As Tabbaa affirms in his conclusion, however, "Conflict, challenge, and controversy, long abhorred by Islamist scholars and dismissed by positivist writers, were at the very foundation of change in medieval Islamic architecture."[5]

Tabbaa's focus on political upheaval also distinguishes him from the majority of art historians who mainly focus on the continuities in Islamic art rather than examining the apparent disjunctions. According to Tabbaa, such art historians, including Sheila Blair, Irene Bierman,* and Eva Baer,* subscribe to "an outmoded essentialist assumption that has been repeatedly questioned but not entirely abandoned." Tabbaa's solution is to embrace the disjunctions of artistic change, in the process producing a more historically nuanced picture of medieval Islamic art. As Tabbaa declares: "It is perhaps time fearlessly to explore these disjunctions and differences across the breadth of Islamic art."[6]

Contribution In Context

In the title of his book, Tabbaa acknowledges a debt to Oleg Grabar's *The Formation of Islamic Art*.[7] First published in 1972, *The Formation of Islamic Art* examines how the development of early Islamic art and architecture reflected broader political, religious, and cultural changes in the Islamic world during the first centuries of Islam. In contrast, *The Transformation of Islamic Art* concentrates on a series of transformations that took place in the eleventh and twelfth centuries, thus advancing and expanding upon the earlier scholarship of Grabar, while at the same time continuing in the historical-contextual approach refined by Grabar in *The Formation*.

A similar approach can be detected in Gülrü Necipoğlu's *The Topkapı Scroll*. There, Necipoğlu argues that the geometrical *girih* mode evolved out of the popularization of theoretical mathematics, optics, and geometry in late-Abbasid Baghdad. Furthermore, Necipoğlu proposes that the *girih* mode was identified as an ideological visual symbol of the early medieval Sunni revival in the eastern Islamic world. Much like Grabar, Necipoğlu explores the sources of the aesthetic and cultural principles that shaped Islamic art and provides insight into the ways in which Islamic visual languages could express aesthetic theories and political identities.

Tabbaa describes Grabar and Necipoğlu's works as important developments in the field and identifies strongly with the ways that both attempted to deal with questions of meaning in Islamic ornament.[8] However, although Tabbaa generally accepts the approaches and interpretive parameters Grabar and Necipoğlu advanced, he also illuminates the field with two key contributions. First, *The Transformation of Islamic Art* has a more limited historical and geographic span than *The Formation of Islamic Art* and *The Topkapi Scroll*, focusing on the artistic and architectural transformations of the Sunni revival in the eleventh and twelfth centuries. Second, Tabbaa differs in his greater emphasis on the transformative power of political and sectarian conflict. Although both Grabar and Necipoğlu examine the impact of political rivalries on the development of Islamic art and architecture, Tabbaa focuses in particular on the ruptures and discontinuities that characterized the Islamic world of the eleventh and twelfth centuries and how these ruptures may have contributed to the emergence of new forms.[9] Tabbaa's perspective is encapsulated best, perhaps, by the questions he proposes at the end of his introduction:

Can we, by problematizing instead of glossing over ruptures, disjunctions, and discontinuities, arrive at a better understanding of the meaning of change in Islamic architecture? And is it not through challenge and controversy that ideas are sharpened, identities reaffirmed, and new concepts created?[10]

Thus, Tabbaa maintains, it is possible to have a more nuanced understanding of changes in Islamic architecture by examining discontinuities against the historical backdrop of contemporaneous political and sectarian conflict.

NOTES

1   Yasser Tabbaa, *The Transformation of Islamic Art During the Sunni Revival*, (London: I.B. Tauris & Co., Ltd. 2001), 167.

2   Tabbaa, *Transformation*, 4-5.

3   Tabbaa, *Transformation*, 7.

4   Tabbaa, *Transformation*, 7.

5   Tabbaa, *Transformation*, 167.

6   Yasser Tabbaa, "Sheila S. Blair, *Islamic Inscriptions* (New York University Press, 1998); Irene A. Bierman, *Writing Signs: The Fatimid Public Text* (University of California Press, 1998); Eva Baer, *Islamic Ornament* (New York University Press, 1998)," *Ars Orientalis* 29 (1999): 182.

7   Tabbaa, *Transformation*, xi.

8   Tabbaa, *Transformation*, 6.

9   Tabbaa, *Transformation*, 6-7 and 77.

10 Tabbaa, *Transformation*, 10.

SECTION 2
IDEAS

MODULE 5
MAIN IDEAS

KEY POINTS

- The Sunni revival was a theological and political movement that sought to reaffirm traditionalist Islam and strengthen the Abbasid caliphate.

- *The Transformation of Islamic Art During the Sunni Revival* examines how the theological tenets and political conflicts that developed during the Sunni revival influenced the art and architecture of the medieval period.

- Each chapter of the book examines how changes in art and architecture reflected parallel changes in the political and religious landscape of the medieval Islamic world.

Key Themes

The Sunni revival is the thread that weaves through the tapestry of Yasser Tabbaa's *The Transformation of Islamic Art During the Sunni Revival*. He defines the Sunni revival as "the theological and political movement that sought to reaffirm traditionalist Islam and reject rationalist thought while declaring allegiance to the Abbasid caliphate and opposing all its enemies."[1]

In order to unpack this definition, it is necessary to turn to the descriptive summary of the Sunni revival furnished by Tabbaa in the opening chapter of his book. At the peak of Abbasid political power in the ninth century, many of the great thinkers and philosophers of the time adopted Mu'tazilism,* a rationalist theology* that believes human reason and intellect can be exercised as a way to know God and can be used to distinguish between good and evil. This stands in opposition to traditionalist theological doctrine, which professes the

> ❝ In the history of Islamic religion the main feature of the century from 850 to 950 was that it became polarized into definite Sunnite and Shī'ite forms. ❞
>
> W. Montgomery Watt, *Islamic Philosophy and Theology*

superiority of God's revelation over reason and was officially sanctioned and supported by the Abbasid state.[2] The Mu'tazilites adhered to a number of principles such as the primacy of free will over predestination and the belief that God is divested of all human attributes.[3] However, the principle that is most relevant to Tabbaa's book pertains to the Mu'tazili belief that God created the Qur'an in order to guide Muslims. As the Mu'tazilites believed, since the Qur'an was not the uncreated and eternal words of God, the Qur'an was open to rational investigation and exegesis.[4]

Traditionalist forces, which galvanized around the ninth century jurist and theologian Aḥmad ibn Ḥanbal,* immediately opposed the doctrines of Mu'tazilism.[5] Ibn Hanbal argued that the Qur'an was uncreated and eternal, and was thus opposed to the rationalist interpretations of the Mu'tazilites. Ibn Ḥanbal was subsequently imprisoned and tortured for opposing Mu'tazilism, which was still the official Abbasid doctrine at the time.[6] However, during the mid-century reign of the Abbasid caliph al-Mutawakkil (847-861), the Abbasids disavowed the Mu'tazili doctrine and began to a sponsor a more traditionalist stance.[7]

The ninth and turn of the tenth centuries also marked the beginning of the political decline of the Abbasid Empire. This decline was precipitated by the development of local governorships under the Abbasid caliphate and greatly accelerated when various dynasties seceded from the caliphate in the tenth century. Two of these, the Umayyads* and the Fatimids of Cairo, even proclaimed their own counter-caliphates. The Abbasids felt particularly threatened by the

Fatimids, who professed Ismaili Shi'ism* and called for an end to the Abbasid state. By the mid-tenth century, the Abbasid domain had been reduced to little more than Iraq, and the Abbasid caliph had been relegated to the position of a nominal figurehead under the control of the Twelver Shiite* Buyids* who reigned 935-1055.[8] In an attempt to reassert their spiritual and political authority, the Abbasids remade their identity by endorsing a traditionalist form of Sunni theology and called for a unity of Sunni dynasties under the umbrella of a revived Sunnism.[9] This political and theological movement towards a reestablishment of Abbasid power through Sunni unity is known as the Sunni revival.

In the early eleventh century, the Abbasid caliph al-Qadir Billah* (reigned 991-1031) began to publicly condemn the Fatimids, Mu'tazilites, and any other polity or sect that did not support the Sunni Abbasids and their traditionalist beliefs. This promotion of Sunni authority was solidified in 1018, when al-Qadir formally adopted a traditionalist Sunni theology known as the Qadiri Creed,* a doctrine influenced by both the strictly traditionalist Hanbali doctrine* and Ash'arism.*[10] Ash'arism can be understood as a theological middle ground between the two principal theological trends at the time, Mu'tazilism and Hanbali traditionalism. Ash'arism originally developed from the writings of the tenth century Sunni theologian Abu'l-Ḥasan al-Ash'ari,* who argued that the Qur'an was eternal and uncreated and professed the superiority of Qur'anic revelation over reason.[11] The Qadiri Creed became the official dogma of the Abbasid caliphate in the first half of the eleventh century and formed the theological cornerstone of the Sunni revival.[12]

The theological tenets of the Sunni revival were promulgated by a succession of Sunni political dynasties such as the Ghaznavids, Seljuqs, Zangids, and Ayyubids, all of whom opposed the enemies of the Abbasid state, in particular the Fatimids and their Ismaili sympathizers. In doing so, these dynasties derived legitimacy from the Abbasid caliphate and demonstrated their loyalty to a policy of unification under a united Sunni Islam.[13] When Tabbaa defines the Sunni revival as a "theological and political movement," therefore, this is precisely what he is referring to: namely, the political unification of dynasties sponsoring Sunni traditionalism against the enemies of the Abbasids.[14]

Thus, in his opening chapter, Tabbaa presents the Islamic world as a series of fragmented polities divided by their political and theological allegiances. On one side are the Abbasids, Ghaznavids, Seljuqs, Zangids, and Ayyubids, all of whom supported the traditionalist Sunni revival and followed the Ash'ari theological doctrine. On the other are the Ismaili Fatimids of Cairo as well as a number of other polities that remained faithful to Mu'tazili doctrine. Understanding this schism is the key to understanding Tabbaa's main argument in *The Transformation of Islamic Art*. As the following section explores, Tabbaa contends that the theological tenets and political factors of the Sunni revival directly contributed to the development of new forms in Islamic art and architecture during this period.

Exploring The Ideas

The Transformation of Islamic Art examines how the theological tenets and political conflicts that developed during the Sunni revival influenced the art and architecture of the medieval period. Specifically, Tabbaa argues that in an attempt to reassert their waning political and spiritual authority, the Abbasids endorsed and disseminated a traditionalist form of Sunni theology, thus facilitating the re-emergence of the Abbasids in a more orthodox image. As part of this religious remaking, the Abbasids created, systematized, and transformed calligraphic, ornamental, and architectural devices in the Abbasid capital of Baghdad. The purpose of this transformation was to create artistic and symbolic forms that expressed and embodied the theological tenets of traditionalist Sunni theology and also functioned as symbols of Abbasid political authority.

The Abbasids then actively sponsored the dissemination of these newly created forms throughout the Islamic world where they were adopted, developed, and further disseminated by a succession of Sunni dynasties such as the Ghaznavids, Seljuqs, Zangids, and Ayyubids. By adopting and developing the forms created by the Abbasids, these Sunni dynasties could demonstrate their allegiance to the Abbasids (which bolstered the temporal and spiritual authority of the Abbasids) and at the same secure a legitimate political and religious status of their own through recognition and appointment from the Abbasid caliphate.

The mutual benefits of this political and artistic alignment accelerated the spread of the newly created forms across the Islamic world, and projected an image of Sunni unity. Furthermore, this structure of reciprocating gestures between the Abbasids and other Sunni polities articulated a strong visual distinction between the traditionalist Sunni's against their main adversaries, the Ismaili Fatimids of Egypt.

As an example, in chapters two and three, Tabbaa examines transformations in Qur'anic writing and public inscriptions. As Tabbaa explains, during the Sunni revival, the Abbasids began to use cursive scripts instead of the old angular *kufic** script to copy Qur'an manuscripts and inscriptions (prior to this, cursive scripts were mainly used for diplomatic and literary writing). According to Tabbaa, the Abbasids made this decision because the greater clarity and legibility of the cursive script reflected the traditionalist Sunni insistence on the clear, explicit, and uncreated nature of the Qur'an. As a result, the cursive script became symbolically charged as a symbol of traditionalist Sunni theology and the Abbasid caliphate. The newly developed cursive script was then disseminated throughout the Islamic world by the Abbasids and a succession of Seljuq and post-Seljuq proponents of the traditionalist Sunni revival, thus achieving a measure of visual unity in the art and architecture sponsored by the Abbasids and other Sunni polities.

41

In contrast, the Fatimids continued to use various forms of *kufic*, a script whose inherent complexity resonated with the Mu'tazili and Ismaili view of the Qur'an as a created text which could be interpreted through rational speculation.[15] The complexity of floriated *kufic* also reflected the Fatimid Ismaili belief that the Quran as a text held two meanings: a surface meaning (*ẓāhir*) and a deeper reading (*bāṭin*).[16] Thus, Tabbaa argues, the creation, use, and dissemination of the symbolically charged cursive script instead of the earlier *kufic* was a strategy intended to distance the Sunni Abbasids, Seljuqs, and Zangids from their Fatimid opponents while at the same time embodying and expressing the tenets of Sunni theology opposed to the esoteric dualism of Ismailism.[17]

Language And Expression

Tabbaa's organization of the material allows his ideas and arguments to emerge in a coherent manner. The book begins with a concise introduction to the political and theological dimensions of the Sunni revival. Tabbaa then dedicates a chapter to each form of Islamic art and architecture to undergo significant change during this period. Each chapter typically begins with a description of the various changes underwent by that particular form, followed by an explanation of how those changes reflected parallel changes in the political and religious landscape of the medieval Islamic world. By structuring his argument in this way, Tabbaa is able to satisfy his primary objective, which is to relate transformations in Islamic art and architecture during the eleventh and twelfth centuries to the religious and political conditions that prevailed during the Sunni revival.

Throughout the work, Tabbaa explains the theological and political concepts that are relevant to his argument in a clear and expressive language, often using images to clarify any technical artistic terminology that he uses. In doing so, Tabbaa ensures that his book has a broad appeal to both specialists of Islamic art and history as well as non–specialists who are new to the field. However, the sheer scope of his argument—which covers the political, religious, and artistic developments in the Islamic world over three centuries—often obliges Tabbaa to focus only on the essential aspects of Islamic theology and political history that are relevant to his book. As such, readers who are interested gaining a more comprehensive understanding of Islamic history and theology can supplement their reading of *The Transformation of Islamic Art* with additional material.

NOTES

1   Yasser Tabbaa, *The Transformation of Islamic Art during the Sunni Revival*, (London: I.B. Tauris & Co., Ltd. 2001), 163.

2   Tabbaa, *Transformation*, 12-13.

3   Tabbaa, *Transformation*, 12-13.

4   Tabbaa, *Transformation*, 12.

5   Tabbaa, *Transformation*, 13.

6   Tabbaa, *Transformation*, 13.

7   Tabbaa, *Transformation*, 13.

8   Tabbaa, *Transformation*, 14.

9   Tabbaa, *Transformation*, 13.

10 Tabbaa, *Transformation*, 15-16.

11 Tabbaa, *Transformation*, 14-15.

12 Tabbaa, *Transformation*, 15-16.

13 Tabbaa, *Transformation*, 165,

14 Tabbaa, *Transformation*, 163.

15 Tabbaa, *Transformation*, 56-57.

16 Tabbaa, *Transformation*, 57

17 Tabbaa, *Transformation*, 8.

MODULE 6
SECONDARY IDEAS

KEY POINTS

- *Transformations in Islamic art during the Sunni revival* did not all occur for the exact same reasons.
- Yasser Tabbaa argues that Qur'anic writing, inscriptions, and the *muqarnas* held specifically religious associations. However, the arabesque *girih* mode and stereotomic* devices lack the same intentionality of use.
- Tabbaa's discussion of textual and monumental scripts has gained the most traction in scholarship.

Other Ideas

The relatively concise length of *The Transformation of Islamic Art During the Sunni Revival* (210 pages including notes, bibliography, and images) reflects Yasser Tabbaa's approach to the subject matter; he rarely indulges any tangents from his main argument and remains focused on his main thesis throughout. Tabbaa also limits the geographical and temporal scope of his study to the territories that were either directly or indirectly affected by the political conflict between the Abbasids and the Fatimids from the tenth to the thirteenth century. As a result, it is difficult to make a clear distinction between primary and secondary ideas. Nevertheless, it is possible to distinguish between the artistic and architectural forms that Tabbaa argues are clear expressions of the theological tenets of the Sunni revival, and those whose religious associations are rather more tenous. Specifically, this latter category of forms pertains to Tabbaa's fourth and sixth chapters; chapter four deals with the development of vegetal and geometric arabesque from the tenth and eleventh centuries, and chapter six examines the proliferation

> 66 Overall, the arabesque seems to lack the intentionality of use, profound iconographic associations, and close links with Abbasid Baghdad that could be demonstrated for the other forms. Its very ubiquity and use in myriad contexts also seem to undermine any specific symbolic associations. 99
>
> Yasser Tabbaa, *The Transformation of Islamic Art During the Sunni Revival*

of five architectural and stereotomic (architectural features consisting of stone masonry cut to specific forms and shapes) devices: foliate arches,* pendant vaults,* stone *muqarnas*, joggled voussoirs,* and interlaced spandrels.*

Exploring The Ideas

Chapters two, three, and five of *The Transformation of Islamic Art* examine how the theological tenets of the Sunni revival were expressed through contemporaneous transformations in calligraphic, ornamental, and architectural forms. Chapters two and three argue that the transformation of Qur'anic writing from the old angular *kufic* to the new proportioned cursive scripts was intended to contrast the exoteric tenets of traditionalist Sunni theology to the esoteric dualism of Ismailism. As Tabbaa argues, the new scripts were more legible and thus more suitable for expressing the "clear and explicit nature of the Word of God."[1]

In chapter five, Tabbaa traces the emergence of the *muqarnas* form (which he defines as a "decorative or structural system in which tiers of repeated small units with discrete geometric shapes are corbelled to form a stair-like or concave pattern or form"[2]) from tenth century eastern Iran to its later applications in eleventh century Baghdad and eventual spread to North Africa and Damascus. Tabbaa proposes that the use of the *muqarnas* in eleventh century

Baghdad followed the triumph of Ash'ari thought and became a symbolic manifestation of the Ash'ari concept of an occasionalist* universe governed by divine causation. Its implementation by other Sunni polities not only promulgated this theological principle but also paid homage to the Abbasid seat of power.[3] In all three of these chapters, therefore, Tabbaa seeks to establish a clear intentionality in the development of artistic and architectural forms as expressions of theological tenets.

However, in chapter four, "The *Girih* Mode: Vegetal and Geometric Arabesque," Tabbaa concedes that the arabesque seems to "lack the intentionality of use" and "profound iconographic associations" that could be demonstrated for the other forms.[4] Furthermore, "its very ubiquity and use in myriad contexts also seem to undermine any specific symbolic associations."[5] At the conclusion of Tabbaa's discussion of stereotomic devices in chapter six, "Stone *Muqarnas* and Other Special Devices," Tabbaa also explains that it is difficult to argue for any specifically religious associations in the absence of relevant contemporary texts to confirm such a hypothesis.[6] Nevertheless, despite the fact that these forms did not reflect theological tenets, these chapters are still crucial to Tabbaa's essential argument, as they still illustrate how newly created forms reflected the political dimensions of the Sunni revival. With regards to the *girih* mode, for example, Tabbaa argues that that the appearance and intense development of the *girih* mode in regions and monuments that are closely linked with the Sunni revival (as well as its marked absence in Fatimid Egypt) bears evidence of the creation and reception of the *girih* mode as a political symbol of the Abbasid caliphate.[7]

Overlooked

Considering the relatively recent date of *The Transformation of Islamic Art's* publication, it is difficult to assess which chapters of the book have been overlooked by scholars in the field. Nevertheless, through an evaluation of later works which have cited Tabbaa's book, it is evident that Tabbaa's research on stereotomic devices have stimulated the least debate, especially in contrast to the debates that have emerged around Tabbaa's hypotheses on the historical development of calligraphy. However, it should be mentioned that this disparity may reflect a wider academic trend in the field of Islamic art, which devotes more scholarly attention to Islamic calligraphy than to the history of carved stone masonry. As such, although Tabbaa's chapter on steretomic devices is integral to his central argument, his research on transformations in Arabic writing has elicited the most positive response from scholars in the field and stimulated the widest debate. As architectural historian Madhuri Desai* writes, "It is in the discussion of textual and monumental scripts that Tabbaa is at his most persuasive, as he traces the development of the new cursive script."[8] Art historian Irvin Cemil Schick* also maintains that, to date, he has "not seen a more convincing alternative" to Tabbaa's argument.[9] Scholars such as Alain George,* Sheila Blair, Bernard O'Kane,* and Schick have also adopted various perspectives on the feasibility of Tabbaa's hypotheses on Islamic calligraphy and either utilized Tabbaa's thesis as a model or offered contrasting opinions.[10]

NOTES

1   Yasser Tabbaa, *The Transformation of Islamic Art during the Sunni Revival*, (London: I.B. Tauris & Co., Ltd. 2001), 50.

2   Tabbaa, *Transformation*, 103.

3   Tabbaa, *Transformation*, 133-4.

4   Tabbaa, *Transformation*, 101.

5   Tabbaa, *Transformation*, 101.

6   Tabbaa, *Transformation*, 162.

7   Tabbaa, *Transformation*, 101.

8   Madhuri Desai, "Review: *The Transformation of Islamic Art during the Sunni Revival* by Yasser Tabbaa," *Journal of the Society of Architectural Historians* 61: 4 (Dec 2002): 564.

9   Irvin Cemil Schick, "The Revival of Kūfī Script during the Reign of Sultan Abdülhamid II," in *Calligraphy and Architecture in the Muslim World*, eds. Mohammad Gharipour and Irvin Cemil Schick (Edinburgh: Edinburgh University Press, 2013), 136.

10   Schick, "The Revival of Kūfī Script," 136; Alain George, *The Rise of Islamic Calligraphy* (Saqi Books: London, 2010), 139; Bernard O'Kane, "Medium and Message in the Monumental Epigraphy of Medieval Cairo," in *Calligraphy and Architecture in the Muslim World*, eds. Mohammad Gharipour and Irvin Cemil Schick (Edinburgh: Edinburgh University Press, 2013), 422; Sheila Blair, *Islamic Calligraphy* (Edinburgh: Edinburgh University Press, 2006), 177.

MODULE 7
ACHIEVEMENT

KEY POINTS

- **Yasser Tabbaa demonstrates how political and religious forces can contribute to the formation of new forms and meanings in Islamic art.**

- **The lack of surviving texts and monuments from Abbasid Baghdad was a limiting factor for Tabbaa.**

- ***The Transformation of Islamic Art During the Sunni Revival* has a broad appeal for scholars and students from diverse disciplines.**

Assessing The Argument

In *The Transformation of Islamic Art During the Sunni Revival*, Yasser Tabbaa satisfies his primary objective of exploring how theological and political developments during the Sunni revival contributed to contemporaneous transformations in Islamic art and architecture. In his introduction, Tabbaa establishes the parameters of the field, demonstrating that there is a significant dearth of studies on how new meanings were created in Islamic artistic and architectural forms during the medieval period.[1] Tabbaa also establishes the temporal and geographical remit of his study, focusing in particular on the artistic and architectural transformations engendered during the Sunni revival. He then collates a wide array of important material, including archaeological evidence, art history data, and primary source texts to demonstrate how calligraphy, inscriptions, geometry, arabesque, *muqarnas*, and stereotomical devices were transformed during the eleventh and twelfth centuries and dispersed through much of the Islamic world. Tabbaa also relates each transformation to the

> ❝ Its two great a priori merits lie in the collation of an array of important material previously scattered through a wide range of diverse sources, and in an analysis that challenges both Islamists and Orientalists by reintroducing the question of agency into a discussion that has often been framed in essentialist and/or evolutionist terms. ❞
>
> Finbarr Barry Flood, "Review of *The Transformation of Islamic Art During the Sunni Revival*"

theological and political forces of the Sunni revival. In doing so, Tabbaa not only examines how art was transformed in a variety of mediums, but also demonstrates how political, religious, and cultural forces can imbue artistic forms with new meaning, thus delivering an original and engaging argument of critical importance to the field of Islamic art and architecture as a whole.

Achievement In Context

As a text that covers the artistic as well as political, cultural, and theological developments across the Islamic world during the medieval period, *The Transformation of Islamic Art* carries a broad appeal to scholars and students from diverse disciplinary backgrounds, including Islamic art, architecture, history, and theology, as well as medieval studies. Furthermore, despite the fact that the primary focus of the book is on the creation, systematization, and dissemination of forms from the Abbasid capital of Baghdad, Tabbaa does not limit the scope of his inquiry to the religious, political, and cultural agents working within that specific geographical and temporal arena. On the contrary, he also explores the cultural policies undertaken by other regional powers in response to developments in the capital (these powers include the Fatimids, Ghaznavids, Seljuqs, Zangids, and

Ayyubids). In doing so, Tabbaa ensures that his text does not remain limited to one particular culture or discipline, but at the same time is not so broad as to lose focus on the Sunni revival.

The methodology and argument of *The Transformation of Islamic Art* also project a broader appeal outside of the temporal framework of the book. Tabbaa's essential thesis in *The Transformation of Islamic Art* is that political and religious conflict stand at the very foundation of change in medieval Islamic art and architecture. Tabbaa delivers his argument by subjecting changes in medieval Islamic art and architecture to historical scrutiny, outlining how political and theological developments during the Sunni revival contributed to the creation and systematization of new forms of art and architecture. Through this contextual approach, he is able to bridge the gap between historical speculation and applied artistry and effectively demonstrate how architecture and the visual arts can become expressions of political and religious dogma. Tabbaa's methodology is important to not only scholars and students specializing in medieval Islamic art and architecture, but also to specialists in other fields seeking a model for how to contextualize artistic and cultural changes.

Limitations

One of the main challenges Tabbaa faced in writing *The Transformation of Islamic Art* was the lack of surviving evidence. A significant portion of his argument is based on confirming the centrality of Baghdad to artistic production during the medieval period. However, in assessing the role of Baghdad, Tabbaa is constrained by the dearth of texts and monuments surviving in Baghdad from the eleventh and twelfth centuries. Thus, even though he was able to travel throughout Iraq to conduct his research, he was still unable to confirm several of his hypotheses against historical evidence.[2] As a result, on a number of occasions throughout his book, Tabbaa is forced to speculate and extrapolate from the surviving evidence of art and architecture created outside of Baghdad and argue that these forms were created in and disseminated from the center.[3] For example, although Tabbaa argues that Baghdad was central to the development of the arabesque, he also acknowledges the near-absence of any surviving monuments in Baghdad before the late twelfth century. As a result, Tabbaa is obliged to construct his argument upon examples nearby in eastern Iran, which may have been a distant reflection of a style that originally emerged in Baghdad.[4]

NOTES

1   Yasser Tabbaa, *The Transformation of Islamic Art during the Sunni Revival*, (London: I.B. Tauris & Co., Ltd. 2001), 4-5.

2   Tabbaa, *Transformation*, xii

3   Tabbaa, *Transformation*, 100, 112, and 122-23.

4   Tabbaa, *Transformation*, 84.

MODULE 8
PLACE IN THE AUTHOR'S LIFE AND WORK

KEY POINTS

- *The Transformation of Islamic Art During the Sunni Revival* is the synthesis and expansion of the ideas explored by Yaseer Tabbaa both during and after his PhD dissertation.

- Throughout his academic career, Tabbaa has explored how historical and contextual factors contributed to the development of Islamic art and architecture.

- *The Transformation of Islamic Art* is the most critically acclaimed work of Tabbaa's academic career.

Positioning

As Yasser Tabbaa explains in his preface, *The Transformation of Islamic Art During the Sunni Revival* arose from two areas of study that he has focused on since he began his career as an art historian: the architecture of Syria and the Jazira between the eleventh and thirteenth centuries, and "the question of meaning in medieval Islamic calligraphic, ornamental, and architectural forms."[1] Specifically, Tabbaa describes how this book represents a metamorphosis from his focused dissertation on the architectural patronage of the mid-twelfth century ruler Nur al-Din Zangi to a synthesis of the wider transformations of medieval Islamic art and architecture during the Sunni revival.[2] This transition was instigated by historian Francis Edward Peters,* who believed that a thesis on the Sunni revival was struggling to emerge from Tabbaa's dissertation.[3] In order to make the necessary transition from a focused study to a comprehensive study of medieval Islamic architecture, Tabbaa had to make three fundamental changes.

> 66 This book grew out of two initially independent
> pursuits that have occupied me since the beginning
> of my career in art history: the architecture of Syria
> and the Jazira between the eleventh and thirteenth
> centuries, and the question of meaning in Islamic
> calligraphic, ornamental, and architectural forms. 99
>
> Yasser Tabbaa, *The Transformation of Islamic Art During the Sunni Revival*

First, the temporal and geographical limits of the investigation had
to be extended well beyond the limits of the original study on Nūr al-
Dīn. Second, some themes deriving from the political and theological
concerns of the Sunni revival had to be expanded, while much formal
analysis had to be curtailed. Third, the chronological approach of the
first project had to be replaced by a typological and thematic approach
that specifically focuses on the question of transformations.[4]

Although *The Transformation of Islamic Art* emerged from his earlier
dissertation, Tabbaa also implemented two major changes: he increased
the scope of his study and established a greater focus on how
theological and political developments during the Sunni revival
contributed to transformations Islamic art and architecture.
Admittedly, this process was "slow and cumulative," and it took Tabbaa
approximately 14 years from the completion of his dissertation to
publish *The Transformation of Islamic Art* in 2001.[5]

During this post-dissertation period, Tabbaa continued to write
on the architecture of Syria and the Jazira between the eleventh and
thirteen centuries and explore the question of meaning in medieval
Islamic art and architecture.[6] In fact, Tabbaa describes how the
publication of a 1985 article on the origins and symbolic meaning
associated with the *muqarnas* dome convinced him of the feasibility of
writing *The Transformation of Islamic Art*.[7] Following the publication of
that article, Tabbaa published three articles exploring the sociopolitical

and religious factors underpinning transformations in Arabic writing during the medieval period, an article on how the art and architecture of Ayyubid Aleppo was influenced by contemporaneous religious and political conflicts, and a book that discusses the expanded patronage of palatial and religious architecture during the Ayyubid period.[8]

The Transformation of Islamic Art can be understood as the culmination, synthesis, and expansion of the research, ideas, and approaches explored by Tabbaa both during and after his PhD dissertation, in that this book stands as an inclusive work that incorporates several strands of inquiry pertaining to how political and theological conflicts contributed to the transformation of Islamic art and architecture. Furthermore, *The Transformation of Islamic Art* not only examines the subjects matters explored by Tabbaa between 1983 and 2001 (transformations in Arabic writing, the *muqarnas* dome, Ayyubid Aleppo, and the patronage of Nūr al-Dīn Zangi), but also expands its parameters to include the art and architecture of the Abbasids, Fatimids, Ghaznavids, and Seljuqs.

Integration

In reviewing the total output of Tabbaa's intellectual career, one can see a relationship between the ideas in *The Transformation of Islamic Art* and those found within Tabbaa's other writings. Both before and after the publication of *The Transformation of Islamic Art*, Tabbaa explored how historical and contextual factors such as politics, theology, culture, and poetics contributed to the development of Islamic art and architecture. Although the geographical and temporal context of his research varies, ranging from tenth century Abbasid calligraphy to Shi'i shrines and from medieval hospitals to Islamic gardens, a coherency of approach can still be observed in his overall corpus of works; Tabbaa consistently challenges positivist and essentialist approaches to Islamic art and adopts theological, linguistic, and sociological modes of interpretation.

One of the main figures to have inspired Tabbaa's theoretical inclinations is his former supervisor and mentor, Oleg Grabar, who famously addressed how religious and cultural factors could influence Islamic art and architecture in his seminal work, *The Formation of Islamic Art*. Although Tabbaa questions some of Grabar's conclusions, he nevertheless accepts Grabar's interpretive parameters and cites Grabar as a major influence on his academic career.[9]

Significance

The Transformation of Islamic Art stands as the most critically acclaimed work of Tabbaa's academic career. This acclaim stems from two main contributions to the field. First, in writing *The Transformation of Islamic Art,* Tabbaa collates a wide range of archaeological evidence and textual sources to provide new information about medieval Islamic art and architecture, still a relatively neglected sector in the field of Islamic art at the time of publication.[10] Second, alongside Grabar and Gülrü Necipoğlu, Tabbaa was one of the first pioneers of a historical-contextual approach to Islamic art.

Tabbaa's original contribution was to examine how the theological tenets of the Sunni revival impacted contemporaneous transformation in calligraphic, ornamental, and architectural forms. Furthermore, Tabbaa stands apart for his emphasis on how new meanings can be created in Islamic art by examining them within the context of contemporary conflicts, challenges, and controversies. For these two contributions, *The Transformation of Islamic Art* is praised as a benchmark in the field of Islamic art and architecture and is his most frequently cited work.

Although a number of historians of Islamic art have been critical of some of the arguments in *The Transformation of Islamic Art*, in general academics have commended Tabbaa for engendering a lively debate and have lauded his book as an exemplary model of how to understand transformations in Islamic art and architecture.[11]

NOTES

1   Yasser Tabbaa, *The Transformation of Islamic Art during the Sunni Revival*, (London: I.B. Tauris & Co., Ltd. 2001), xi.

2   Tabbaa, *Transformation*, xi.

3   Tabbaa, *Transformation*, xi.

4   Tabbaa, *Transformation*, xi.

5   Tabbaa, *Transformation*, xi.

6   Yasser Tabbaa, "The *Muqarnas* Dome: Its Origin and Meaning," *Muqarnas* 3 (1985); Yasser Tabbaa, "Monuments with a Message: Propagation of Jihad under Nur al-Din," in *The Meeting of Two Worlds: Cultural Exchange Between East and West During the Period of the Crusades*, ed. V. Goss and C. Vézar-Bornstein (Kalamazoo, Michigan: Medieval Institute Publications, 1986); Yasser Tabbaa, "Geometry and Memory in the *Madrasat* al-Firdaws in Aleppo, 1235," in *Theories and Principles of Design in the Architecture of Islamic Societies*, ed. Margaret Sevcenko (Cambridge, MA: Aga Khan Program Publications, 1988); Yasser Tabbaa, "Survivals and Archaisms in the Architecture of Northern Syria, ca. 1080-ca. 1150," *Muqarnas* 10 (1993).

7   Tabbaa, *Transformation*, xi.

8   Yasser Tabbaa, "The Transformation of Arabic Writing, I. Quranic Calligraphy," *Ars Orientalis* 21 (1991); Yasser Tabbaa, "Circles of Power: Palace, Citadel and City in Ayyubid Aleppo," *Ars Orientalis* 23 (1993); Yasser Tabbaa, "The Transformation of Arabic Writing, II. The Public Text," *Ars Orientalis* 24 (1994); Yasser Tabbaa, "Canonicity and Control: The Sociopolitical Underpinnings of Ibn Muqla's Reform," *Ars Orientalis* 29 (1999).

9   Tabbaa, *Transformation*, 6 and 77; Robert Hillenbrand, "Oleg Grabar: The Scholarly Legacy," *Journal of Art Historiography* 6 (June 2012): 24, fn 110, accessed August 18, 2017, https://arthistoriography.files.wordpress.com/2012/05/hillenbrand.pdf.

10 Finbarr Barry Flood, "Review of *The Transformation of Islamic Art during the Sunni Revival* by Yasser Tabbaa," *caa.reviews* (November 4, 2002): accessed August 16, 2017, doi: 10.3202/caa.reviews.2002.76.

11 Flood, "Review of *The Transformation*"; Irvin Cemil Schick, "The Revival of Kūfī Script during the Reign of Sultan Abdülhamid II," in *Calligraphy and Architecture in the Muslim World*, eds. Mohammad Gharipour and Irvin Cemil Schick (Edinburgh: Edinburgh University Press, 2013), 132.

SECTION 3
IMPACT

MODULE 9
THE FIRST RESPONSES

KEY POINTS

- Shortly after the book's publication, a number of scholars criticized Yassser Tabbaa for his selective use of sources and limited scope of enquiry.

- Tabbaa and art historian Sheila Blair disagree over a number of issues pertaining to the historical development of Arabic writing.

- Neither Tabbaa nor Blair have modified their views following their debate.

Criticism

Shortly after the publication of Yasser Tabbaa's *The Transformation of Islamic Art During the Sunni Revival*, a number of scholars in the field of Islamic art and architecture published reviews of the text. Although the reviews were generally favorable, a number of criticisms have been leveled against Tabbaa's selective use of sources as well as his lack of evidence.

In Madhuri Desai's review, she criticizes Tabbaa for crediting changes and the exchange of ideas solely to a politically motivated policy of Sunni religious expansion. By taking the Sunni revival as its central theme, Desai explains, Tabbaa is "locked into a stance" where the transformation of forms is attributed mainly to the agency of religious and political leaders.[1] As a result, Tabbaa "gives little consideration to other social and economic conditions and events that might have brought about changes and facilitated the geographical spread of artistic and architectural formal devices and technologies."[2] Such conditions and events could include trade and pilgrimage routes,

> ❝ Tabbaa deserves much credit for successfully bringing history back into the study of the architecture of the Near and Middle East in this amply illustrated and elegant book. ❞
>
> Madhuri Desai, "Review of *The Transformation of Islamic Art During the Sunni Revival*," *Journal of the Society of Architectural Historians*

which may have facilitated the exchange of ideas outside of an explicitly politically motivated context. As an example, Desai cites the research of Jonathan Bloom,* who argues that trade and pilgrimage connections enabled architectural elements such as the *muqarnas* to reach Egypt via the Red Sea from Mecca.[3]

Desai also describes the symbolic connections Tabbaa proposes between theological tenets and transformations as "not always convincing" due to a lack of adequate textual material to support such interpretations.[4] A third criticism is directed towards Tabbaa's characterization of the art and architecture of the medieval period as specifically "Islamic"; that is to say, as art and architecture produced under the patronage of Islamic dynasties as a consequence of Islamic religious and political motives.[5] As Desai points out, innovations in art and architecture in the countries of the Middle and Near East and North Africa in the eleventh, twelfth, and thirteenth centuries could have also been produced through interaction and exchange between populations of different religious and ethnic affiliations.[6] Desai's criticisms suggest that a more complete and nuanced picture of transformations in Islamic art during the medieval period might have been drawn by exploring varied trajectories of social interaction and evolutions of Islamic art beyond the history of the caliphal and political institutions of Islam.

Finnbar Barry Flood* also highlights several points of contention. For example, Tabbaa argues that the Zangid use of polylobed arches* reflected a conscious adoption of forms newly imbued with specific sectarian connotations.[7] However, Flood suggests that their use in the Zangid monuments of the Jazira in the twelfth century may actually be evidence of regional continuity. As Flood explains, polylobed arches existed in Sassanian* Iraq and appear in Abbasid monuments such as the palace at Ukhaydir.*[8] To this end, the existence of polylobed arches in Zangid monuments might be seen as a continuation of established architectural traditions rather than as newly created forms that were adopted from Baghdad.

A second criticism pertains to evidence. One of the arguments that is central to Tabbaa's thesis is that the art and architecture of the Sunni revival was markedly different to that of their main opponents, the Fatimids of Egypt. Tabbaa argues, for example, that the *muqarnas* form was proliferated across the medieval visual landscape of the Sunni revival, but was restricted to a relatively minor context in Fatimid monuments. However, Flood suggests that such differences and disjunctions may actually reflect the nature of the surviving material. Flood gives the example of Norman Sicily (which had strong cultural affinities to Fatimid Egypt), where the *muqarnas* form can be found in a significant number of monuments, raising the possibility that the *muqarnas* was popular in Fatimid palace architecture (no examples of which have survived).[9] Although Flood concedes that a disjunction between the use of *muqarnas* in Fatimid religious and secular architecture does not necessarily negate Tabbaa's thesis (and could even support it), it also points to "complexities in the dissemination of artistic forms to which a simple Sunni-Shi'i opposition would not do justice."[10] Flood also points out that there were a significant number of forms that were common to the Fatimid and Abbasid domains, such as figural ornamentation in the secular arts of both cultural spheres.[11] Such commonalities reflect a shared artistic culture that Tabbaa rarely explores and bear evidence of the transmission of certain forms across religious and cultural boundaries.

A third critique can be found in Sheila Blair and Jonathan Bloom's article "The Mirage of Islamic Art," published a year after *The Transformation of Islamic Art.* In "The Mirage," Blair and Bloom criticize Tabbaa's narrow geographical scope.[12] According to Blair and Bloom, Tabbaa's exclusive focus upon the Arab lands "tends to skew the larger picture" and overlooks the possible contributions of Iran and Central Asia to developments in the artistic and architectural landscape of the Islamic medieval period.[13]

Despite their criticisms, both Desai and Flood are highly complementary of Tabbaa's research and ambition in writing *The Transformation of Islamic Art.* Specifically, Flood commends Tabbaa for his innovative approach, for his collation of primary sources, and for raising a debate that "can only be healthy for the field as a whole."[14] Desai also praises Tabbaa for "successfully bringing history back into the study of the architecture of the Near and Middle East" and for departing from essentialist and ethno-nationalist interpretations.[15] Furthermore, Desai describes *The Transformation of Islamic Art* as "an important step in the right direction."[16]

Responses

A significant dialogue did not emerge between Tabbaa and the critics of *The Transformation of Islamic Art* in the period immediately following the book's publication. However, Blair and Bloom's's critique of *The Transformation of Islamic Art* in "The Mirage" continues from an earlier dialogue established between Tabbaa and Blair. In Blair's *Islamic Inscriptions* (published in 1998), she criticizes "The Transformation of Arabic Writing, I," Tabbaa's 1991 article exploring transformations in Arabic calligraphy during the medieval period.[17] In this article, which eventually formed the basis for *The Transformation of Islamic Art*, Tabbaa associates a series of transformations in Qur'anic calligraphy and public inscriptions with the contemporaneous reassertion of political authority and religious orthodoxy under the Abbasid caliphate.

However, according to Blair, "attempts to impute political motivations to stylistic changes, however enticing, are wrong, for they are not grounded in an accurate knowledge of the epigraphic material. They overlook significant specimens, omit material that does not fit with preconceived hypotheses, and disregard events that occurred elsewhere."[18] In Blair's opinion, Arabic public writing followed a stylistic continuum and did not emerge as a symbolic form canonized in response to rival polities. Blair proposes that Fatimid floriated *kufic* may find its origins in earlier Ikhshidid* inscriptions[19] and that cursive inscriptions can be traced back to east Iranian coinage.[20]

Tabbaa responds to Blair's criticisms in his review of Blair's *Islamic Inscriptions*. Tabbaa explains that his work does not necessarily omit material, but is selective in order to limit his scope to material that relates to the transformation of public and official inscriptions. Tomb inscriptions, for example, "clearly belong to a lower and less public type of patronage, outside my main field of investigation."[21] Responding to Blair's observation that tomb inscriptions appear in the floriated *kufic* style outside of the Fatimid realm (which undermines Tabbaa's argument that floriated *kufic* was symbolically associated with the Fatimids), he acknowledges their existence, but responds that it was the Fatimids who "systematized this script and recast it as the official public script of the dynasty."[22] As such, their appearance outside of the Fatimid realm does not necessarily contradict his claim that the Fatimids consciously appropriated and disseminated floriated *kufic* script through the medium of public inscriptions.

Tabbaa also rebukes Blair's suggestion that his interpretation of the switch from the angular to cursive script is based on Irene Bierman and Ibrahim Jum'ah's* work, claiming that his work is only "tangentially" related to Jum'ah's.[23] Furthermore, unlike Bierman, Tabbaa's work does not rely as much on Fatimid esoteric texts.[24] Rather, Tabbaa claims that his work is founded on Max van Berchem* and Ernst Herzfeld,* acknowledging that "If anything, I have attempted to historicize their sweeping conclusions by pointing out differential change in various regions and by more intimately linking the process to contemporary historical sources and treatises."[25]

Finally, in his review, Tabbaa reaffirms the contrasting approaches taken by Blair and himself towards the development of Arabic writing over time. Whereas Tabbaa seeks to rationalize changes and ruptures in the history of Arabic writing over time, according to Blair, "Arabic writing changed continuously and seamlessly through internal processes whose course can be described and classified but not explained."[26] Tabbaa considers the persistent sense of continuity, which is a hallmark of Blair's writing, to be a derivative of "an outmoded essentialist assumption that has been repeatedly questioned but not entirely abandoned."[27] In offering a solution, Tabbaa encourages his contemporaries to "fearlessly" embrace the "disjunctions and differences across the breadth of Islamic art," in the process producing a more historically nuanced picture of medieval Islamic art.[28]

Conflict And Consensus

Neither Tabbaa nor Blair has modified their views following this dialogue. In Blair's monograph on the historical development of the Arabic scripts, *Islamic Calligraphy*, published five years after *The Transformation of Islamic Art*, Blair comments on "the limited scope of Tabbaa's inquiry" in his book. Blair maintains that this limited scope overlooks other specimens of calligraphy outside of Qur'an manuscripts.[29] Furthermore, Blair suggests that Tabbaa's correlation of cursive scripts with the theological tenets of Sunni Islam is "based on negative evidence."[30] In order to support this criticism, Blair cites the example of the libraries of Fatimid Cairo, which were in possession of manuscripts written in the cursive script. The existence of these manuscripts in the Fatimid collection seemingly contradicts the arguments Tabbaa furnishes in his second and third chapter of *The Transformation of Islamic Art*, which assert that the reformed cursive scripts were used by the Abbasids in order to distance the Sunni Abbasids and the Seljuq–Zangid state from their Fatimid adversaries while manifesting the exoteric tenets of traditionalist Sunni theology. Emphatically, Blair writes: "In my view, the canonization of round scripts (and also geometry) had nothing to do with religious sectarianism in the tenth century."[31]

NOTES

1   Madhuri Desai, "Review: *The Transformation of Islamic Art during the Sunni Revival* by Yasser Tabbaa," *Journal of the Society of Architectural Historians* 61: 4 (Dec 2002): 564.

2   Desai, "Review," 564.

3   Desai, "Review," 564.

4   Desai, "Review," 564.

5   Desai, "Review," 565.

6   Desai, "Review," 565.

7   Finbarr Barry Flood, "Review of *The Transformation of Islamic Art during the Sunni Revival* by Yasser Tabbaa," *caa.reviews* (November 4, 2002): accessed August 16, 2017, doi: 10.3203/caa.reviews.2002.76. Flood, "Review of *The Transformation*."

9   Flood, "Review of *The Transformation*."

10 Flood, "Review of *The Transformation*."

11 Flood, "Review of *The Transformation*."

12 Sheila S. Blair and Jonathan M. Bloom, "The Mirage of Islamic Art: Reflections on the Study of an Unwieldy Field," *The Art Bulletin*, 85, 1 (2003): 156-57.

13 Blair and Bloom, "Mirage," 172.

14 Flood, "Review of *The Transformation*."

15 Desai, "Review," 565.

16 Desai, "Review," 565.

17 Yasser Tabbaa, "The Transformation of Arabic Writing, I. Quranic Calligraphy," *Ars Orientalis* 21 (1991), 119-147.

18 Sheila S. Blair, Islamic Inscriptions (New York: New York University Press, 1998), 7; Yasser Tabbaa, "Sheila S. Blair, Islamic Inscriptions (New York University Press, 1998); Irene A. Bierman, Writing Signs: The Fatimid Public Text (University of California Press, 1998); Eva Baer, Islamic Ornament (New York University Press, 1998)," Ars Orientalis 29 (1999): 181.

19 Blair, *Islamic Inscriptions*, 58-59.

20 Blair, *Islamic Inscriptions*, 16.

21 Tabbaa. "Sheila S. Blair, *Islamic Inscriptions*," 181.

22 Tabbaa. "Sheila S. Blair, *Islamic Inscriptions*," 181.

23 Blair, *Islamic Inscriptions*, 57; Tabbaa, "Review of *Islamic Inscriptions*," 181.

24 Tabbaa. "Sheila S. Blair, *Islamic Inscriptions*," 181.

25 Tabbaa. "Sheila S. Blair, *Islamic Inscriptions*," 181.

26 Tabbaa. "Sheila S. Blair, *Islamic Inscriptions*," 181.

27 Tabbaa. "Sheila S. Blair, *Islamic Inscriptions*," 182.

28 Tabbaa, "Sheila S. Blair, *Islamic Inscriptions*," 182.

29 Sheila Blair. *Islamic Calligraphy* (Edinburgh: Edinburgh University Press, 2006), 175.

30 Blair. *Islamic Calligraphy*, 175.

31 Blair. *Islamic Calligraphy*, 177.

MODULE 10
THE EVOLVING DEBATE

KEY POINTS

- Art historians Alain George and Bernard O'Kane question whether the cursive scripts systemized under the Abbasids held any ideological connotations.

- Despite the criticisms *The Transformation of Islamic Art During the Sunni Revival* has received, Yasser Tabbaa has been praised for rejecting essentialist, Orientalist, and ethno-nationalist approaches to Islamic art.

- *The Transformation of Islamic Art* is cited as a reliable source of information on the art and architecture of the medieval Islamic period.

Uses And Problems

Following the initial reviews of Yasser Tabbaa's *The Transformation of Islamic Art During the Sunni Revival*, more scholars in the field began to respond to his book. A number of them echoed the doubts of Madhuri Desai, Finbarr Barry Flood, and Sheila Blair, but also brought their own criticisms to the debate. For the most part, the academic responses to *The Transformation of Islamic Art* did not seek to completely reject Tabbaa's ideas; on the contrary, many scholars expressed admiration for his historical–contextual approach. However, a number of scholars did point out some of the weaknesses in Tabbaa's argument or adopted positions that conflict with his central ideas.

In his book *The Rise of Islamic Calligraphy*, Alain George seriously questions whether the new cursive scripts developed under the Abbasids held any ideological connotations. He writes: "Thus even

> ❝ Thus even though Ibn Muqla was involved in several
> anti-Shi'ite actions, his role in the long process leading
> to the establishment of a standard Qur'anic text should
> not be overplayed. When we look at the manuscript
> record, it seems just as difficult to associate the New
> Style with an assertion of Sunni orthodoxy. ❞
>
> Alain George, *The Rise of Islamic Calligraphy*

though Ibn Muqla* [who, alongside Ibn al-Bawwab,* canonized the cursive scripts] was involved in several anti-Shi'ite actions, his role in the long process leading to the establishment of a standard Qur'anic text should not be overplayed. When we look at the manuscript record, it seems just as difficult to associate the New Style with an assertion of Sunni orthodoxy."[1]

George also points out that a collection of cursive calligraphy written by Ibn Muqla and Ibn al-Bawwab, together with the pens sharpened by their hands, were held in the Fatimid treasury. This would imply that the Fatimids were not so averse to the cursive script developed under the Abbasids at all; on the contrary, the Fatimids appear to have held the work of Ibn Muqla and Ibn al-Bawwab in high esteem, which contradicts Tabbaa's essential thesis that the cursive scripts were developed under the Abbasids as ideological symbols of a traditionalist Sunni Islam.[2]

Bernard O'Kane also questions Tabbaa's proposition that the cursive script *naskh** held ideological connotations.[3] In *The Transformation of Islamic Art*, Tabbaa argues that the *naskh* script was symbolically charged as a symbol of the resurgent Sunni revival.[4] However, O'Kane points out that examples of *naskh* can also be found in a number of Fatimid contexts in Cairo, such as on a cupboard that was formerly in the al-Salih Tala'i mosque* and on a cenotaph (a tomb erected in honor of an individual whose body lies elsewhere) in the al-Husayn Mosque.*[5] Once again, the appearance of *naskh* in Fatimid buildings appears to negate Tabbaa's essential thesis that the *naskh* script was canonized as an ideological symbol of the Sunni revival.

Schools Of Thought

Considering the relatively recent date of its publication, it is still too early to identify any new schools of thought that have been inspired by *The Transformation of Islamic Art*. This endeavor is also hampered by the comparatively small size of the field of Islamic art and architecture in relation to other fields of art history and the humanities. Nevertheless, following its publication, *The Transformation of Islamic Art* endeared a number of scholars to Tabbaa's historical-contextual approach. Scholars of Islamic art and architecture such as Flood and Desai praised Tabbaa for rejecting essentialist, Orientalist, and ethno-nationalist approaches to Islamic art and for constructing an argument based on theological, political, sociological, and semiotic modes of an interpretation.[6] As Flood anticipates, the debates engendered by Tabbaa's work are bound to stimulate a lively discussion that "can only be healthy for the field as a whole."[7]

In light of this positive reception, it is highly likely that *The Transformation of Islamic Art* will continue to push students and scholars away from discussions of Islamic art framed in essentialist or evolutionist terms and instead encourage a mode of analysis that examines how artistic concepts can be created through political and theological controversy.

In Current Scholarship

A number of scholars have developed and advanced the project started by Tabbaa in *The Transformation of Islamic Art*. Historians of Islamic art such as Stephennie Mulder,* Caroline Olivia M. Wolf,* Cynthia Robinson, and Hana Taragan* have continued to explore the connections between religious and political ideologies and the monuments of the medieval Islamic world. Throughout their works, *The Transformation of Islamic Art* is cited as a reliable source of information for the history, art and architecture of the medieval Islamic period.[8] Furthermore, Tabbaa's book is endorsed as recommended reading for its critical treatment of the historiography of Islamic art.

Another vocal supporter of *The Transformation of Islamic Art* is art historian Irvin Cemil Schick. For Schick, Tabbaa's book represents a constructive alternative to essentialist and positivist studies of architectural inscriptions. Such studies typically focus upon an inscription's content, style, and aesthetic value at the expense of any discussion of how these attributes may express or embody certain political or religious concepts. Tabbaa is thus commended for seeking to identify the cultural processes by which meaning was produced within inscriptions.[9] Tabbaa's approach resonates particularly with Schick, who co-edited the volume *Calligraphy and Architecture in the Muslim World* with the intention of treating architectural calligraphy as something "more than pure text."[10]

In his article in the same volume ("The Revival of Kūfī Script during the Reign of Sultan Abdülhamid II*"), Schick explicitly cites Tabbaa's methodology as an influence and applies a similar approach to explain aesthetic shifts in calligraphy during the late Ottoman period. Just as Tabbaa sought to contextualize the transition from the angular to the cursive script against the historical framework of the Sunni revival, so too does Schick seek to relate the Ottoman revival of the *kufic* script with contemporaneous political and religious developments.

NOTES

1   Alain George, *The Rise of Islamic Calligraphy* (Saqi Books: London, 2010), 139.

2   George, *The Rise of Islamic Calligraphy*, 134-143.

3   Bernard O'Kane, "Medium and Message in the Monumental Epigraphy of Medieval Cairo," in *Calligraphy and Architecture in the Muslim World*, eds. Mohammad Gharipour and Irvin Cemil Schick (Edinburgh: Edinburgh University Press, 2013), 422.

4   Yasser Tabbaa, *The Transformation of Islamic Art during the Sunni Revival*, (London: I.B. Tauris & Co., Ltd. 2001), 50.

5   O'Kane, "Medium and Message", 422.

6   Finbarr Barry Flood, "Review of *The Transformation of Islamic Art during the Sunni Revival* by Yasser Tabbaa," caa.reviews (November 4, 2002): accessed August 16, 2017, doi: 10.3202/caa.reviews.2002.76; Madhuri Desai, "Review: *The Transformation of Islamic Art during the Sunni Revival* by Yasser Tabbaa," *Journal of the Society of Architectural Historians* 61: 4 (Dec 2002): 565.

7   Flood, "Review of *The Transformation*."

8   Stephennie Mulder, "The Mausoleum of Imam Al-Shafiʿi," *Muqarnas* 23 (2006), 42; Hana Taragan, "The Tomb of Sayyidnā ʿAlī in Arṣūf: The Story of a Holy Place," *Journal of the Royal Asiatic Society*, Third Series, 14, No. 2 (July 2004), 87; Cynthia Robinson, "Marginal Ornament: Poetics, Mimesis, and Devotion in the Palace of the Lions," *Muqarnas*, Frontiers of Islamic Art and Architecture: Essays in Celebration of Oleg Grabar's Eightieth Birthday 25 (2008): 210; Caroline Olivia M. Wolf, "'The Pen Has Extolled Her Virtues': Gender and Power within the Visual Legacy of Shajar al-Durr in Cairo," in *Calligraphy and Architecture in the Muslim World*, eds. Mohammad Gharipour and Irvin Cemil Schick (Edinburgh: Edinburgh University Press, 2013), 210.

9   Irvin Cemil Schick, "The Revival of Kūfī Script during the Reign of Sultan Abdülhamid II," in *Calligraphy and Architecture in the Muslim World*, eds. Mohammad Gharipour and Irvin Cemil Schick (Edinburgh: Edinburgh University Press, 2013), 132.

10 Irvin Cemil Schick, "Introduction," in *Calligraphy and Architecture in the Muslim World*, eds. Mohammad Gharipour and Irvin Cemil Schick (Edinburgh: Edinburgh University Press, 2013), 6.

MODULE 11
IMPACT AND INFLUENCE TODAY

KEY POINTS

- *The Transformation of Islamic Art During the Sunni Revival* has been described as a timely and important contribution to the field of Islamic art and architecture.

- Yasser Tabbaa challenges Orientalists, positivists, essentialists, ethno-nationalists, and art historians of an earlier generation.

- In laying down this challenge, Tabbaa is supported by a number of art historians of his generation.

Position

Yasser Tabbaa's *The Transformation of Islamic Art During the Sunni Revival* remains one of the most important texts in the field of Islamic art and architecture, both for the wealth of information it provides on the art and architecture of the medieval Islamic period and for its innovative approaches to the study of Islamic art. As a resource, scholars view *The Transformation of Islamic Art* as a great work of primary evidence collation and analysis, and the text is often used as a reliable reference for the historiography, history, art, and architecture of the Abbasid, Zangid, Fatimid, Seljuq, and Ayyubid periods.[1] In terms of its approach, the text has been widely praised for critiquing and rejecting positivist, essentialist, and Orientalist narratives of Islamic art and for reintroducing a contextual approach to interpreting historical data, an approach that encourages a broad range of theological, sociological, and semiotic modes of interpretation.[2]

Still, some of Tabbaa's main conclusions are controversial. Scholars such as Sheila Blair, Madhuri Desai, Finbarr Barry Flood, Alain

> ❝ It is worth noting here that Tabbaa's hypothesis has not been universally accepted, however, I, for one, have not seen a more convincing alternative to date. ❞
>
> Irvin Cemil Schick, "The Revival of Kūfī Script during the Reign of Sultan Abdülhamid II," *Calligraphy and Architecture in the Muslim World*

George, and Bernard O'Kane have expressed a range of opinions regarding Tabbaa's essential thesis; some have pointed out inconsistencies in Tabbaa's argument, while others have offered alternative readings of the development of Islamic art during the eleventh and twelfth centuries.[3] However, despite these criticisms, a number of scholars have supported Tabbaa's arguments and have cited *The Transformation of Islamic Art* as being a seminal influence on their work. Irvin Cemil Schick, for example, acknowledges some of the negative reviews of the text, but remains supportive of Tabbaa's essential thesis: "It is worth noting here that Tabbaa's hypothesis has not been universally accepted, however, I, for one, have not seen a more convincing alternative to date."[4] The fact that Schick pronounced his support as recently as 2013, almost 12 years after Tabbaa published his book, testifies to the continued relevance of *The Transformation of Islamic Art* to current debates in the field.

The commendations, criticisms, and debates that *The Transformation of Islamic Art* has inspired following its publication bear witness to the importance of this work. *The Transformation of Islamic Art* still serves as a strong methodological counterpoint to ahistorical approaches to the analysis of visual culture in the Islamic tradition and articulates an innovative, intellectual, and highly influential interpretation of transformations in Islamic art. In this respect, Tabbaa's work is not only a "game-changer" in its own right, but in terms of the evolution of the field, *The Transformation of Islamic Art* stands as a signpost of generational growth.

Interaction

In the introduction to *The Transformation of Islamic Art*, Tabbaa challenges a number of archaeologists, Orientalists, aestheticians, and art historians. First, Tabbaa highlights an interpretive vacuum in the work of archaeologists and art historians such as K.A.C. Creswell, J. Michael Rogers, and Michael Meinecke.[5] This group of scholars generally rejected the possibility that Islamic art and architecture could be an expression or application of Islamic dogma. This principle was constructed upon the belief that Muslim artists and architects did not leave behind a significant body of texts and documents that dealt with questions of meaning. As a result, Creswell and others were disinclined to take up the question of meaning, preferring instead to focus on the taxonomical* description of monuments.[6]

Tabbaa also criticizes Orientalists and art historians of an earlier generation who saw the main features of Islamic art as timeless reflections of an Oriental or Islamic spirit.[7] Scholars adopting an ethno-nationalist approach are also subject to critique; despite the fact that they reject the pan-Islamic perspective of Orientalism, they rather problematically propose that Islamic art is linked to innate ethnic or national character traits.[8]

Tabbaa is also highly critical of a school he collectively refers to as "a group of aestheticians and Muslim fundamentalists."[9] According to Tabbaa, this group, including Titus Burckhardt, Martin Lings,* and Seyyed Hossein Nasr, adopt an essentialist perspective that sees Islamic art as a reflection of timeless Islamic religious and cultural values, and thus overlook the possibility that the meaning of Islamic art changed over time. Furthermore, they fail to explore whether other meanings, political, theological, or otherwise, were projected onto Islamic art throughout history.[10] In response, Tabbaa challenges the aforementioned scholars to study developments in Islamic art and architecture with due consideration of their political, religious, and social history. In doing so, it is possible to investigate how new meanings were produced within definable moments of profound political, theological, and cultural change.[11]

The Continuing Debate

In laying down this challenge, Tabbaa is supported by several of historians of Islamic art and architecture including Desai and Flood. In his review of Tabbaa's work, Flood describes *The Transformation of Islamic Art* as "an analysis that challenges both Islamists and Orientalists by reintroducing the question of agency into a discussion that has often been framed in essentialist and/or evolutionist terms."[12] Similarly, Desai writes that "Tabbaa deserves much credit for successfully bringing history back into the study of the architecture of the Near and Middle East."[13]

As for the scholars that Tabbaa has challenged, thus far no concerted or coordinated response has emerged from the groups of individuals that Tabbaa refers to as Orientalists, ethno-nationalists, and "Muslim fundamentalists." However, Sheila Blair (whom Tabbaa accuses of ignoring the possible religious or political significance of artistic form) has rejected Tabbaa's essential thesis. As Blair writes: "In my view, the canonization of round scripts (and also geometry) had nothing to do with religious sectarianism in the tenth century."[14] Considering the fact that both Tabbaa and Blair share a similar field of interest (Islamic inscriptions and epigraphy, Islamic calligraphy, and the Islamic architecture of Iran and Iraq), it is natural for there to be issues of contention between the scholars, and it is likely that further debates and responses will emerge as the field continues to expand.

NOTES

1   Stephennie Mulder, "The Mausoleum of Imam Al-Shafi'i," *Muqarnas* 23 (2006), 42; Hana Taragan, "The Tomb of Sayyidnā 'Alī in Arṣūf: The Story

of a Holy Place," *Journal of the Royal Asiatic Society*, Third Series, 14, No. 2 (July 2004), 87; Cynthia Robinson, "Marginal Ornament: Poetics, Mimesis, and Devotion in the Palace of the Lions," *Muqarnas*, Frontiers of Islamic Art and Architecture: Essays in Celebration of Oleg Grabar's Eightieth Birthday 25 (2008): 210; Caroline Olivia M. Wolf, "'The Pen Has Extolled Her Virtues': Gender and Power within the Visual Legacy of Shajar al-Durr in Cairo," in *Calligraphy and Architecture in the Muslim World*, eds. Mohammad Gharipour and Irvin Cemil Schick (Edinburgh: Edinburgh University Press, 2013), 210.

2   Madhuri Desai, "Review: *The Transformation of Islamic Art during the Sunni Revival* by Yasser Tabbaa," *Journal of the Society of Architectural Historians* 61: 4 (Dec 2002): 565; Finbarr Barry Flood, "Review of *The Transformation of Islamic Art during the Sunni Revival* by Yasser Tabbaa," *caa.reviews* (November 4, 2002): accessed August 16, 2017, doi: 10.3202/caa.reviews.2002.76.

3   Desai, "Review" 563-65; Flood, "Review of *The Transformation*; Alain George, *The Rise of Islamic Calligraphy* (Saqi Books: London, 2010), 139; Bernard O'Kane, "Medium and Message in the Monumental Epigraphy of Medieval Cairo," in *Calligraphy and Architecture in the Muslim World*, eds. Mohammad Gharipour and Irvin Cemil Schick (Edinburgh: Edinburgh University Press, 2013): 416-30.

4   Irvin Cemil Schick, "The Revival of Kūfī Script during the Reign of Sultan Abdülhamid II," in *Calligraphy and Architecture in the Muslim World*, eds. Mohammad Gharipour and Irvin Cemil Schick (Edinburgh: Edinburgh University Press, 2013), 136.

5   Yasser Tabbaa, *The Transformation of Islamic Art during the Sunni Revival*, (London: I.B. Tauris & Co., Ltd. 2001), 4.

6   Tabbaa, *The Transformation*, 4.

7   Tabbaa, *The Transformation*, 4.

8   Tabbaa, *The Transformation*, 4.

9   Tabbaa, *The Transformation*, 5.

10 Tabbaa, *The Transformation*, 5.

11 Tabbaa, *The Transformation*, 9-10 and 167.

12 Flood, "Review of *The Transformation*."

13 Desai, "Review," 565.

14 Sheila Blair, *Islamic Calligraphy* (Edinburgh: Edinburgh University Press, 2006), 177.

MODULE 12
WHERE NEXT?

KEY POINTS

- *The Transformation of Islamic Art During the Sunni Revival* is likely to have a continued influence on future studies of medieval Islamic art and architecture.

- There are currently a significant number of scholars working on topics similar to Yasser Tabbaa's subject matter.

- *The Transformation of Islamic Art* has changed the way scholarship has approached and conceptualized moments of change in medieval Islamic architecture.

Potential

It is likely that both the subject matter and approach of Yasser Tabbaa's *The Transformation of Islamic Art During the Sunni Revival* will continue to affect future debates on Islamic art. Regarding the former, the research and data presented in the book currently serve as reliable points of reference for scholars working in the field today, and this trend is projected to continue until the unlikely event that Tabbaa's data is proved incorrect. As for Tabbaa's approach, a similar influence can be anticipated. In Irvin Cemil Schick's recent article on the revival of the *kufic* script during the Ottoman period, he describes the potential applicability of Tabbaa's approach to understanding other changes in calligraphic styles across time and space. For example, Tabbaa's approach could be used to rationalize the emergence of *thuluth** and *naskh* under the 1447–1512 reign of Ottoman Sultan Bayezid II,* or to understand the development and spread of the *nasta'liq** script from the fifteenth century onwards.[1]

> ❝ Can we, by problematizing instead of glossing over ruptures, disjunctions, and discontinuities, arrive at a better understanding of the meaning of change in Islamic architecture? And is it not through challenge and controversy that ideas are sharpened, identities reaffirmed, and new concepts created? ❞
>
> Yasser Tabbaa, *The Transformation of Islamic Art During the Sunni Revival*

In part, the impact of Tabbaa's argument in his book will depend on whether alternative theories of the Sunni revival emerge in the future and whether these theories negate or concur with Tabbaa's hypothesis. At the same time, regardless of whether Tabbaa's arguments hold true, *The Transformation of Islamic Art* has been applauded for advancing the study of Islamic art beyond Orientalist, positivist, and essentialist approaches, and for investigating how new meanings— political, religious, or otherwise—were attributed to Islamic art and architecture over time. As Finbarr Barry Flood writes, such an investigation is bound to engender a lively discussion and debate, which "can only be healthy for the field as a whole."[2] Most recently, scholars such as Schick have also emphasized the importance of following this approach:

Meaning and form mutually inflect each other in a unique way in Islamic calligraphy, and only giving due consideration to this verbal-visual intertext can lead to a genuine appreciation of this art. Calligraphy *means*—that is, calligraphy conveys meaning—through both its verbal content and its form.[3]

If the discipline of art history continues to shift in this direction, it can be predicted with a considerable degree of certainty that *The Transformation of Islamic Art During the Sunni Revival* will continue to influence and engender further debates in the field of Islamic art and architecture.

Future Directions

Compared to other fields of art history, the field of Islamic art and architecture is still relatively small and understudied. As such, it is difficult to say which art historians are likely to carry on Tabbaa's work in the future. Nevertheless, there are a significant number of scholars specializing in the art and architecture of the Islamic medieval period who are likely to continue working on projects similar to Tabbaa's, and are also likely to advance, update, and even abrogate Tabbaa's essential thesis. These scholars include Stephennie Mulder, Bernard O'Kane, Schick, Gülrü Necipoğlu, Hana Taragan, Sheila Blair, Jonathan Bloom, Robert Hillenbrand,* Eva Hoffman,* Alain George, and Scott Redford.* Most recently, Schick co-edited *Calligraphy and Architecture of the Muslim World,* a volume (including articles written by Schick, O'Kane, and Blair) dedicated to exploring how calligraphic inscriptions have partaken in the infusion of meaning into architectural spaces.[4] As Schick emphasizes in the introduction, calligraphy is still woefully neglected by art historians, and very little has been done to understand "what calligraphy is, what calligraphy means, and what calligraphy does."[5] *The Transformation of Islamic Art* paved the way for such studies by treating calligraphy and inscriptions as artistic devices that are more than just pure decoration or text. In this regard, *The Transformation of Islamic Art* can be considered a defining work in the history of Islamic art and architecture; it apprised and updated the scholarly works of the past and influenced the future directions of the field.

Summary

In both subject matter and approach, *The Transformation of Islamic Art* makes original contributions to the field of Islamic art and architecture. It challenges essentialist, Orientalist, positivist, and ethno-nationalist readings of Islamic art and offers thought-provoking alternatives that incorporate theological, political, sociological, and semiotic modes of interpretation. *The Transformation of Islamic Art* also represents the first attempt to investigate the impact of the theological tenets of the Sunni revival on contemporaneous transformations in calligraphic, ornamental, and architectural forms. Furthermore, Tabbaa's book demonstrates that the relatively neglected sector of the Medieval Islamic period is of critical importance in understanding the historical development of Islamic art. As such, *The Transformation of Islamic Art* is a seminal text in the historiography of Islamic art and architecture, in that it has changed the way scholarship has approached and conceptualized moments of change in medieval Islamic architecture. Although Tabbaa's arguments are not widely accepted, they have engendered a lively debate that is likely to continue into the future. As Flood observes, such a debate "can only be healthy for the field as a whole," for as Tabbaa asks at the close of the introduction to his book, "Is it not through challenge and controversy that ideas are sharpened, identities reaffirmed, and new concepts created?"[6]

NOTES

1   Irvin Cemil Schick, "The Revival of Kūfī Script during the Reign of Sultan Abdülhamid II," in *Calligraphy and Architecture in the Muslim World*, eds. Mohammad Gharipour and Irvin Cemil Schick (Edinburgh: Edinburgh University Press, 2013), 132.

2   Finbarr Barry Flood, "Review of *The Transformation of Islamic Art during the Sunni Revival* by Yasser Tabbaa," *caa.reviews* (November 4, 2002): accessed August 16, 2017, doi: 10.3202/caa.reviews.2002.76.

3   Schick, "The Revival of Kūfī Script," 135.

4   Irvin Cemil Schick, "Introduction," in *Calligraphy and Architecture in the Muslim World*, eds. Mohammad Gharipour and Irvin Cemil Schick (Edinburgh: Edinburgh University Press, 2013), 1.

5   Schick, "Introduction," 3.

6   Flood, "Review of *The Transformation*"; Yasser Tabbaa, *The Transformation of Islamic Art during the Sunni Revival*, (London: I.B. Tauris & Co., Ltd. 2001), 10.

GLOSSARY

GLOSSARY OF TERMS

Abbasids (r. 750–1258): a powerful Muslim caliphate that claimed descent from Abbas ibn Abd al-Muttalib (d. 653), the uncle of the Prophet Muhammad (d. 632), who had adopted him as a child.

Al-Husayn Mosque: a mosque originally built in Cairo in 1154. It holds the head of Husayn bin Ali (d. 680), the grandson of the Prophet Muhammad.

Al-Salih Tala'i Mosque: a late Fatimid-era mosque commissioned by the Fatimid vizier Al-Salih Tala'I ibn Ruzik in 1160.

Arabesque: a style of decoration commonly used in Islamic art which consists of intertwining tendrils and abstract foliage motifs.

Ash'arism: a traditionalist school of Islamic theology founded by Imam Abu al-Hasan al-Ash'ari (d. 935/6). The Ash'arites held that the Qur'an was eternal and that revelation was more fundamental than reason as the source of ultimate truth.

Ayyubids (r. 1171–1260): a Muslim dynasty that came to power under the leadership of the Zangid general Salah al-Din Ayyubi (r. 1169-93). The Ayyubids brought an end to Fatimid rule in 1171.

Buyids (r. 935–1055): a dynasty of Daylamite origin (Northern Iran) that ruled over southern and western Iran and Iraq.

Caliphate: a state or territory ruled under the political and religious authority of an Islamic leader known as the caliph.

Crusades (1096-1291): a series of Christian military expeditions against the Muslims initiated to establish control of holy sites considered sacred by both faiths.

Divine Oneness and Unity: the fundamental understanding that God is the sole creator and ruler, and that all aspects of existence have their origin in God alone.

Essentialism: a perspective that holds that all artistic and architectural devices hold certain attributes and meanings, which are essential to its identity. For example, all Islamic architecture embodies the spirit of Islamic revelation.

Ethno-nationalism: a perspective that interprets the main features of art as a reflection of ethnic or national character traits. For example, the characteristic features of Islamic art are interpreted as being "Turkish" or "Persian" instead of "Islamic" or "Ottoman."

Fatimids (r. 909-1171): an Ismaili Muslim caliphate founded by Abdullah al-Mahdi Billah (d. 934). The Fatimids ruled over North Africa, Sicily, Palestine, and Syria.

Foliate Arch: an arch consisting of a series of indented leaf-shaped or circular spaces.

Ghaznavids (r. 977-1186): a Muslim dynasty of Turkic origin. At their greatest extent the Ghaznavids ruled large parts of Iran, Afghanistan, much of Transoxiana, and northwestern India.

***Girih* mode:** a style of geometry characterized by the use of interlaced straps and star patterns.

Gulf War (1990–91): an international conflict initiated by Iraqi
president Saddam Hussain's (reigned 1979–2003) invasion of Kuwait
on August 1, 1990.

Hanbali Doctrine: a theological tradition closely associated with the
school of jurisprudence established by Ahmad ibn Hanbal (d. 855). The
Hanbalites emphasized the uncreatedness of the Qur'an and were
opposed to rational arguments in matters of dogma.

Ikhshidids (r. 935–969): a Muslim dynasty that ruled over Egypt. The
Ikhshidid dynasty was brought to an end when the Fatimids
conquered Fustat in 969.

Interlaced Spandrel: the decorated space between the curve of an
arch and its rectangular frame.

Iran–Iraq War (1980–88): a military conflict between Iran and Iraq
lasting from September 1980 to August 1988. It began when Iraqi
president Saddam Hussein ordered Iraqi forces to invade Western Iran.

Iranian Revolution (1979–80): a series of mass popular civil
insurrections in Iran that overthrew the ruling monarch, Shah
Mohammed Reza Pahlavi and established an Islamic republic. Also
known as the Islamic Revolution or the 1979 Revolution.

Ismaili Shi'ism: a term that refers to adherents of a branch of Shia
Islam who accept Isma'il ibn Ja'far (d. 755) as the appointed successor
to Imam Ja'far al-Sadiq (d. 765).

Jazira: a region that is now made up of part of northern Iraq, eastern
Turkey and northeastern Syria.

Joggled Voussoir: a method of construction that uses interlocking blocks of masonry in two contrasting colours.

Kufic: an early angular calligraphic script typically used to copy Qur'anic verses.

Late Antiquity: a term used to describe the time of transition from the decline of the Roman Empire to the emergence and early expansion of Islam. Typically, this period is given as 250-750.

Mu'talizism: a rationalist school of Islamic theology that flourished in the cities of Basra and Baghdad during the eighth and tenth centuries. Mu'tazilites believed in the created nature of the Qur'an and posited that the injunctions of God were accessible to rational thought and reason.

Muqarnas: a system of projecting niches resembling stalactites. The *muqarnas* is typically used for zones of transition and for architectural decoration.

Naskh: a cursive calligraphic script typically used for writing the Qur'an from the eleventh century onwards.

Nasta'liq: a cursive calligraphic script thought to be developed in fifteenth century Iran.

Occasionalism: the belief that the universe is sustained and governed through divine causation. Within the occasionalist philosophical framework, God maintains the order of the universe by preserving and creating the universe from one instant to another through a constant process of annihilation and recreation.

Orientalism: a concept that points to the cultural representation, false imagination, and stereotyping of Middle Eastern peoples and cultures in Western literature, media, and art.

Pendant Vault: a form of vault in which large sculpted ornaments descend from a vaulted ceiling.

Perennialism: a philosophical perspective that underlines the fundamental truths shared by the world's religions. In discussing Islamic art and architecture, perennialist philosophers emphasize the aesthetic unity and symbolic meanings of form across time and space.

Polylobed Arches: arches decorated with a series of carved scallops or curves.

Positivism: an empirical approach to Islamic art and architecture that limits interpretation and restricts speculation on meaning and metaphysics.

Qadiri Creed: an edict passed by the Abbasid caliph al-Qadir in 1018 that promoted the traditionalist Sunni theological doctrine of the Sunni revival and condemned the Ismailis and Mu'tazilites.

Rationalist Theology: a theology that believes that human reason and intellect can be exercised as a way to know God and can be used to distinguish between good and evil. This stands in opposition to the traditionalist theological doctrine, which professes the superiority of God's revelation over reason.

Sassanian Dynasty (224–651): an Iranian dynasty established by King Ardashir I (r. 224–241). At its peak, the Sassanian territory stretched from the River Euphrates to the River Indus.

Sectarianism: intense devotion to a particular sect or group.

Seljuqs (r. 1037–1307): a Turkic Muslim dynasty that ruled parts of Central Asia, Syria, Palestine, Iran, and Mesopotamia from the eleventh to the fourteenth centuries.

Soviet Invasion of Afghanistan (1979–1989): the invasion of Afghanistan in December 1979 by troops from the Soviet Union.

Stereotomic: architectural features consisting of stone masonry cut to specific forms and shapes.

Sunni: a denominative term referring to Muslims who regard the first four caliphs—Abu Bakr (d. 634), Umar ibn al-Khattab (d. 644), Uthman ibn Affan (d. 656), and Ali ibn Abi Talib (d. 661)—as the legitimate successors of the Prophet Muhammad (d. 632).

Syrian Civil War (2011–): an armed conflict in Syria, fought primarily between the ruling government of President Bashar al-Assad against forces opposed to his rule.

Taxonomical: in art and architecture, an approach that categorizes, analyses, and explores the origin and development of forms but does not concern itself with interpreting the possible political or religious meaning of those forms.

Thuluth: a cursive calligraphic script typically used for Qur'anic chapter headings and architectural inscriptions.

Topkapi Scroll: a late fifteenth-century compendium of architectural drawings used for the generation of two and three-dimensional patterns on walls and in vaults.

Traditionalist Theology: a theological doctrine that professes the superiority of God's revelation over reason.

Twelver Shi'ism: the principal branch of Shi'i Islam. The Twelver Shi'i's follow the twelve imams they consider to be the rightful successors of the Prophet Muhammad, beginning with the Prophet's son-in law and cousin, Ali ibn Abi Talib (d. 661), and ending with Muhammad ibn al-Hasan (b. 869) who is believed to be the Mahdi (a spiritual messiah who will restore justice before the end of the world).

Ukhaydir: an early Abbasid (second half of the eighth century) Islamic palace in Iraq located approximately 200 kilometers south of Baghdad.

Umayyads (r. 661–750): an early Muslim dynasty that ruled the Islamic caliphate. The Umayyad period is considered formative to the development of Islamic art and architecture.

US-led Invasion of Afghanistan (2001–): an invasion of Afghanistan triggered in response to the September 11, 2001 terrorist attacks on America. The US accused the Taliban, the ruling power in Afghanistan, of protecting Osama Bin Laden, who was believed to be behind the terrorist attack.

US-led Invasion of Iraq (2003–2011): an armed conflict that began with the invasion of Iraq by a US led coalition. The coalition believed that the Iraqi president Saddam Hussain was harboring weapons of mass destruction.

Zangids (r. 1127–1222): a Muslim dynasty that ruled over Syria northern Iraq and Syria.

PEOPLE MENTIONED IN THE TEXT

Sultan Abdülhamid II (1842-1918) ruled as Ottoman sultan from 1876-1909. In an attempt to exert effective control over the fracturing Ottoman state, Abdülhamid initiated major social, education, and administrative reforms.

Mehmet Aga-Oglu (1896-1941) was one of the first pioneers to establish Islamic art history as an academic discipline. Born to Turkish parents in Yerevan, Armenia, Aga-Oglu held positions at the National Museum in Constantinople and the Detroit Institute of Arts and held the first chair in the history of Islamic art in America at the University of Michigan.

Abu al-Hasan al-Ash'ari (873/4-935/6) was a Muslim theologian born in Baghdad. He founded a theological school that professed the uncreated nature of the Qur'an and emphasized the superiority of Qur'anic revelation over reason.

Sultan Bayezid II (1447-1512) ruled as Sultan of the Ottoman Empire from 1447-1512. Bayezid consolidated and expanded Ottoman territory and was a cultured patron of the arts.

Eva Baer (1920-2017) was a professor emerita of the Department of Art History, Islamic Art Division, at Tel Aviv University. Baer specialized in Islamic metalwork, ornament, and iconography.

Ibn al-Bawwab (full name Abu al-Hasan Ali Ibn Hilal Ibn al-Bawwab, d. 1022 or 1031) was one of the major pioneers of Islamic calligraphy. Born in Baghdad, al-Bawwab refined the rules of Ibn Muqla's six scripts and canonized the aesthetic principles that governed the rules of calligraphy.

Max van Berchem (1863–1921) was a Swiss epigraphist and historian of Islamic art and archaeology. He was the founding scholar of the study of Arabic epigraphy, and published widely on the Arabic inscriptions of Syria, Egypt, Palestine, and part of Anatolia.

Irene Bierman (1942–2015) was professor emerita of art history at the University of California, Los Angeles. Bierman's critically acclaimed work *Writing Signs: The Fatimid Public Text* offered insights into how propagandist meanings were embedded in Fatimid inscriptions and buildings.

Al-Qadir Billah (947–1031, r. 991–1031) was the twenty-fifth Abbasid caliph. He pursued a religious policy of religious orthodoxy inspired by Hanbali and Ash'ari thought.

Sheila Blair (b. 1948) is an American professor of Islamic art who currently teaches Islamic art and architecture at Boston College. Blair specializes in the arts of Iran and Central Asia, Islamic calligraphy, and Islamic inscriptions.

Jonathan Bloom is co-chair of the Norma Jean Calderwood University Professorship of Islamic and Asian Art at Boston College. His research explores the history and development of the minaret, the history of paper, and the art and architecture of the Fatimids.

Titus Burckhardt (1908–1984) was a leading proponent of perennialism and traditionalist thought. Burckhardt's publications on Islamic art, including *Sacred Art in East and West, Fez: City of Islam,* and *Art of Islam*, examine the relationship between metaphysics and aesthetics in the art and architecture of sacred traditions.

K.A.C. Creswell (full name Sir Keppel Archibald Cameron Creswell, 1879–1974) was an English archaeologist and architectural historian. He is one of the earliest pioneers of the study of early Islamic architecture and wrote two seminal works in the field: *Early Muslim Architecture* and *The Muslim Architecture of Egypt*.

Muayyad Basim Demerji is a former director general of antiquities in Iraq in the 1980s.

Madhuri Desai is associate professor of art history and Asian studies in the Department of Art History at Penn State. Desai's main research interests include are in South Asian architectural and urban history.

Richard Ettinghausen (1906–1979) was a German-born historian of Islamic art. Ettinghausen worked as both lecturer and curator of Islamic art and architecture and was one of the founding fathers of the discipline of Islamic art history in the United States.

Finbarr Barry Flood is the William R. Kenan Jr. Professor of the Humanities at the New York University Institute of Fine Arts and College of Arts and Sciences. Flood's fields of expertise include the art and architecture of the Islamic world, the cross-cultural dimensions of Islamic material culture, Orientalism, and art historical historiography, methodology, and theory.

Alain George is senior lecturer in art history at the University of Edinburgh and author of *The Rise of Islamic Calligraphy*. George specializes in the arts of the Islamic world, Qur'anic calligraphy and Islamic manuscripts.

Oleg Grabar (1929–2011) was a French-born art historian and archaeologist of Islamic art and architecture. Grabar explored the nature and meanings of the characteristic forms of Islamic art and expanded the intellectual scope of the discipline of Islamic art and architecture by introducing theological, sociological, and semiotic modes of interpretation.

Ahmad ibn Hanbal (780–855) was a Muslim theologian and jurist born in Baghdad. He founded one of the four orthodox schools of Islamic jurisprudence.

Ernst Herzfeld (1879–1948) was a German archaeologist, philologist, and historian in the field of Near Eastern Studies. His major contributions include architectural studies of Samarra, Damascus, and Northern Syria and the publication of architectural inscriptions in Assyrian, Old Persian, Middle Persian, and Arabic.

Robert Hillenbrand has taught at the Department of Fine Art, University of Edinburgh, since 1971 and was awarded a chair of Islamic art in 1989. Hillenbrand retired in December 2007 but is currently an Honorary Professorial Fellow in the department of Islamic and Middle Eastern Studies (IMES). His research interests include Islamic architecture and Islamic painting with a particular specialism in Iran and Umayyad Syria.

Eva Hoffman is assistant professor in the Department of Art and Art History at Tufts University. Hoffman's research interests include Islamic painting and the art and architecture of the medieval Mediterranean world.

Ibrahim Jum'ah was an Egyptian scholar who composed a study of the development of *kufic* writing on stone in Egypt during the first five centuries of Islam.

Martin Lings (1909–2005) was an acclaimed scholar, author, historian, translator, metaphysician and poet. He is best known for his works on Islam and Sufism, which include *A Moslem Saint of the Twentieth Century: Shaikh Ahmad Al-Alawi: His Spiritual Heritage and Legacy, Shakespeare in the Light of Sacred Art, What is Sufism?, The Quranic Art of Calligraphy and Illumination, Muhammad: His Life Based on the Earliest Sources*, and *Symbol and Archetype: A Study of the Meaning of Existence*.

Michael Meinecke (1941–1995) was an archaeologist and historian of Islamic art born in Vienna. Meinecke taught at the University of Hamburg from 1977–80 and took over the post of director of the Museum of Islamic Art in the Pergamon Museum in 1988.

Stephennie Mulder is associate professor of Islamic art and architecture at the University of Texas, Austin. Her research interests include the art and architecture of Shi'ism and the intersections between art, spatiality, and sectarian relationships in Islam.

Ibn Muqla (full name Abu Ali Muhammad ibn Ali ibn Muqla, 885/6–940) was an Abbasid vizier (a high official and minister of state) and one of the foremost calligraphers of the Abbasid period. Born in Baghdad, Ibn Muqla established a proportional system of calligraphy and developed the form of six major calligraphic scripts.

Seyyed Hossein Nasr (b. 1933) is a philosopher, historian, and scholar of comparative religions. His published works on Islamic art include *Islamic Art and Spirituality* and *Sacred Art in Persian Culture*.

Gülrü Necipoğlu (b. 1956) is the Aga Khan Professor of Islamic Art and the director of the Aga Khan Program for Islamic Architecture at Harvard University's Department of History of Art and Architecture.

She specializes in Ottoman art and architecture, the question of meaning and aesthetics in Islamic art, ornament and geometric design, and Islamic historiography and methodology and is the author of *Architecture, Ceremonial Power: The Topkapi Palace* (1991), *The Topkapi Scroll: Geometry and Ornament in Islamic Architecture* (1995), and *The Age of Sinan: Architectural Culture in the Ottoman Empire* (2005).

Bernard O'Kane is professor of Islamic art and architecture at the American University in Cairo. He is the author of several key works in the field including *Studies in Persian Art and Architecture, Early Persian Painting: Kalila and Dimna Manuscripts of the Late Fourteenth Century,* and *The World of Islamic Art*.

Francis Edward Peters (b. 1927) is professor emeritus of history, religion, and Middle Eastern studies at New York University. Peters specializes in the history of religion and the comparative study of Judaism, Christianity, and Islam.

Scott Redford is an archaeologist and the Nasser D. Professor of Islamic Art at the School of Oriental and African Studies, University of London. He is the author of a number of books on Seljuq art and architecture, including *Legends of Authority: The 1215 Seljuk Inscriptions of Sinop Citadel Turkey, Victory Inscribed: The Seljuk Fetihname on the Citadel Walls of Antalya* (co-author), and *Landscape and the State in Medieval Anatolia: Seljuk Gardens and Pavilions of Alanya, Turkey*.

Cynthia Robinson is professor of Art History at Cornell University. She is the author of *Imagining the Passion in a Multi-Confessional Castile* and *In Praise of Song: The Making of Courtly Culture in al-Andalus and Provence*. Robinson specializes in cultural contact and interchange in the Mediterranean world between 1000 and 1500.

J. M. Rogers (b. 1935) is the author of numerous articles and books on Islamic art, architecture, and history. He was the inaugural holder of the Nasser D. Khalili Chair of Islamic Art and Archaeology at the University of London's School of Oriental and African Studies and previously worked as the deputy keeper in the Department of Oriental Antiquities at the British Museum in charge of Islamic collections.

Irvin Cemil Schick (b. 1955) is a Turkish art historian specializing in Ottoman calligraphy. He is the co-editor of *Calligraphy and Architecture in the Muslim World* and author of several articles on Ottoman calligraphy including "The Iconicity of Islamic Calligraphy in Turkey" and "Taczâde Risâlesine Göre Sülüs Hattına Dair Bazı Istılâhat" ("Some Thuluth Script Terminology According to the Treatise of Taczâde").

Priscilla P. Soucek is John L. Loeb Professor in the History of Art at the New York Institute of Fine Arts. Her main research interests include Persian and Arabic manuscripts, portraiture, and the history of collecting.

Issa Sulaiman was the former Director General of Antiquities in Iraq.

Hana Taragan teaches Islamic art and architecture in the Department of Art History at Tel Aviv University. Her fields of research include Umayyad art and architecture, Muslim-Crusader encounters, and the art and architecture of the Ayyubid and Mamluk periods in Egypt, Jazira, and Syria.

Caroline Olivia M. Wolf is a PhD candidate at Rice University. Her research primarily focuses on issues of immigration and identity in the visual culture and built environment of Latin America. Wolf has also published research on the Mamluk Sultan Shajar al-Durr (d. 1257).

Nur al-Din Zangi (1118–1174, r. 1146–1174) was a Muslim ruler in Syria and the Jazira. He came to power upon the death of his father Imad al-Din Zangi (d. 1146), who was the patriarch of the Zangid dynasty.

WORKS CITED

WORKS CITED

Blair, Sheila S. *Islamic Calligraphy*. Edinburgh: Edinburgh University Press, 2006.

Islamic Inscriptions. New York: New York University Press, 1998.

Blair, Sheila S. and Jonathan M. Bloom. "The Mirage of Islamic Art: Reflections on the Study of an Unwieldy Field." *The Art Bulletin*, 85, 1 (2003): 152-84.

Burckhardt, Titus. *The Art of Islam: Language and Meaning*. London: World of Islam Festival Trust, 1976.

Desai, Madhuri. "Review: The Transformation of Islamic Art During the Sunni Revival by Yasser Tabbaa." *Journal of the Society of Architectural Historians* 61:4 (Dec., 2002): 563-565.

Flood, Finbarr Barry. "Review of *The Transformation of Islamic Art During the Sunni Revival* by Yasser Tabbaa." *Caa.reviews* (November 4, 2002). Accessed June 4th, 2014. doi:10.3202/caa.reviews.2002.76.

George, Alain. *The Rise of Islamic Calligraphy*. Saqi Books: London, 2010.

Grabar, Oleg. *The Formation of Islamic Art*. New Haven, CT: Yale University Press, 1973.

Hillenbrand, Robert. "Oleg Grabar: The Scholarly Legacy." *Journal of Art Historiography* 6 (June 2012). Accessed August 18, 2017. https://arthistoriography.files.wordpress.com/2012/05/hillenbrand.pdf.

Mervin, Sabrina, and Yasser Tabbaa. *Najaf: The Gate of Wisdom*. Paris: UNESCO, 2014.

Mulder, Stephennie. "The Mausoleum of Imam Al-Shafi'i." *Muqarnas* 23 (2006): 15-46.

Nasr, Seyyed Hossein. *Islamic Art and Spirituality*. Albany: SUNY Press, 1987.

Necipoğlu, Gülru. "The Concept of Islamic Art: Inherited Discourses and New Approaches." In *Islamic Art and the Museum*, edited by Benoît Junod, Georges Khalil, Stefan Weber and Gerhard Wolf, 57-75. London, Saqi Books, 2012.

The Topkapi Scroll—Geometry and Ornament in Islamic Architecture. Santa Monica, CA: The Getty Center for the History of Art and the Humanities, 1995.

O'Kane, Bernard. "Medium and Message in the Monumental Epigraphy of Medieval Cairo." In *Calligraphy and Architecture in the Muslim World*, edited by Mohammad Gharipour and Irvin Cemil Schick, 416-430. Edinburgh: Edinburgh University Press, 2013.

Robinson, Cynthia. "Marginal Ornament: Poetics, Mimesis, and Devotion in the Palace of the Lions." *Muqarnas* 25, Frontiers of Islamic Art and Architecture: Essays in Celebration of Oleg Grabar's Eightieth Birthday (2008): 185-214.

Schick, Irvin Cemil. "Introduction." In *Calligraphy and Architecture in the Muslim World*, edited by Mohammad Gharipour and Irvin Cemil Schick, 1-9. Edinburgh: Edinburgh University Press, 2013.

"The Revival of Kūfī Script during the Reign of Sultan Abdülhamid II." In *Calligraphy and Architecture in the Muslim World*, edited by Mohammad Gharipour and Irvin Cemil Schick, 119-138. Edinburgh: Edinburgh University Press, 2013.

Tabbaa, Yasser. "The Architectural Patronage of Nūr al-Dīn, 1146-1174." PhD diss., New York University, 1983.

"Canonicity and Control: The Sociopolitical Underpinnings of Ibn Muqla's Reform." *Ars Orientalis* 29 (1999): 91-100.

Constructions of Power and Piety in Medieval Aleppo. Pennsylvania: State University Press, 1997.

"Circles of Power: Palace, Citadel and City in Ayyubid Aleppo." Ars Orientalis 23 (1993): 181-200.

"Geometry and Memory in the *Madrasat* al-Firdaws in Aleppo, 1235." In *Theories and Principles of Design in the Architecture of Islamic Societies*, edited by Margaret Sevcenko, 23-34. Cambridge, MA: Aga Khan Program Publications, 1988.

"Invented Pieties: The Rediscovery and Rebuilding of the Shrine of Sayyida Ruqayya in Damascus, 1975-2006." *Artibus Asiae,* 67, no. 1, Pearls from Water. Rubies from Stone. Studies in Islamic Art in Honor of Priscilla Soucek. Part II (2007): 95-112.

"Monuments with a Message: Propagation of Jihad under Nur al-Din." In *The Meeting of Two Worlds: Cultural Exchange Between East and West During the Period of the Crusades,* edited by V. Goss and C. Vézar-Bornstein, 223-241. Kalamazoo, Michigan: Medieval Institute Publications, 1986.

"The *Muqarnas* Dome: Its Origin and Meaning." *Muqarnas* 3 (1985): 61-76.

"Sheila S. Blair, *Islamic Inscriptions* (New York University Press, 1998); Irene A. Bierman, *Writing Signs: The Fatimid Public Text* (University of California Press, 1998); Eva Baer, Islamic Ornament (New York University Press, 1998)." *Ars Orientalis* 29 (1999): 180-82.

"Survivals and Archaisms in the Architecture of Northern Syria, ca. 1080-ca. 1150." *Muqarnas* 10 (1993): 29-41.

"The Transformation of Arabic Writing, I. Quranic Calligraphy." *Ars Orientalis* 21 (1991): 119-147.

"The Transformation of Arabic Writing, II. The Public Text." *Ars Orientalis* 24 (1994): 119-148.

The Transformation of Islamic Art During the Sunni Revival. London: I. B. Tauris & Co, 2001

Taragan, Hana. "The Tomb of Sayyidnā 'Alī in Arṣūf: The Story of a Holy Place." *The Journal of the Royal Asiatic Society* 14, Third Series, No. 2 (July 2004): 83-102.

Watt, Montgomery W. *Islamic Philosophy and Theology*, Edinburgh: Edinburgh University Press, 1985.

Wolf, Caroline Olivia M. "'The Pen Has Extolled Her Virtues': Gender and Power within the Visual Legacy of Shajar al-Durr in Cairo." In *Calligraphy and Architecture in the Muslim World*, edited by Mohammad Gharipour and Irvin Cemil Schick, 199-216. Edinburgh: Edinburgh University Press, 2013.

THE MACAT LIBRARY
BY DISCIPLINE

AFRICANA STUDIES

Chinua Achebe's *An Image of Africa: Racism in Conrad's Heart of Darkness*
W. E. B. Du Bois's *The Souls of Black Folk*
Zora Neale Huston's *Characteristics of Negro Expression*
Martin Luther King Jr's *Why We Can't Wait*
Toni Morrison's *Playing in the Dark: Whiteness in the American Literary Imagination*

ANTHROPOLOGY

Arjun Appadurai's *Modernity at Large: Cultural Dimensions of Globalisation*
Philippe Ariès's *Centuries of Childhood*
Franz Boas's *Race, Language and Culture*
Kim Chan & Renée Mauborgne's *Blue Ocean Strategy*
Jared Diamond's *Guns, Germs & Steel: the Fate of Human Societies*
Jared Diamond's *Collapse: How Societies Choose to Fail or Survive*
E. E. Evans-Pritchard's *Witchcraft, Oracles and Magic Among the Azande*
James Ferguson's *The Anti-Politics Machine*
Clifford Geertz's *The Interpretation of Cultures*
David Graeber's *Debt: the First 5000 Years*
Karen Ho's *Liquidated: An Ethnography of Wall Street*
Geert Hofstede's *Culture's Consequences: Comparing Values, Behaviors, Institutes and Organizations across Nations*
Claude Lévi-Strauss's *Structural Anthropology*
Jay Macleod's *Ain't No Makin' It: Aspirations and Attainment in a Low-Income Neighborhood*
Saba Mahmood's *The Politics of Piety: The Islamic Revival and the Feminist Subjec*t
Marcel Mauss's *The Gift*

BUSINESS

Jean Lave & Etienne Wenger's *Situated Learning*
Theodore Levitt's *Marketing Myopia*
Burton G. Malkiel's *A Random Walk Down Wall Street*
Douglas McGregor's *The Human Side of Enterprise*
Michael Porter's *Competitive Strategy: Creating and Sustaining Superior Performance*
John Kotter's *Leading Change*
C. K. Prahalad & Gary Hamel's *The Core Competence of the Corporation*

CRIMINOLOGY

Michelle Alexander's *The New Jim Crow: Mass Incarceration in the Age of Colorblindness*
Michael R. Gottfredson & Travis Hirschi's *A General Theory of Crime*
Richard Herrnstein & Charles A. Murray's *The Bell Curve: Intelligence and Class Structure in American Life*
Elizabeth Loftus's *Eyewitness Testimony*
Jay Macleod's *Ain't No Makin' It: Aspirations and Attainment in a Low-Income Neighborhood*
Philip Zimbardo's *The Lucifer Effect*

ECONOMICS

Janet Abu-Lughod's *Before European Hegemony*
Ha-Joon Chang's *Kicking Away the Ladder*
David Brion Davis's *The Problem of Slavery in the Age of Revolution*
Milton Friedman's *The Role of Monetary Policy*
Milton Friedman's *Capitalism and Freedom*
David Graeber's *Debt: the First 5000 Years*
Friedrich Hayek's *The Road to Serfdom*
Karen Ho's *Liquidated: An Ethnography of Wall Street*

John Maynard Keynes's *The General Theory of Employment, Interest and Money*
Charles P. Kindleberger's *Manias, Panics and Crashes*
Robert Lucas's *Why Doesn't Capital Flow from Rich to Poor Countries?*
Burton G. Malkiel's *A Random Walk Down Wall Street*
Thomas Robert Malthus's *An Essay on the Principle of Population*
Karl Marx's *Capital*
Thomas Piketty's *Capital in the Twenty-First Century*
Amartya Sen's *Development as Freedom*
Adam Smith's *The Wealth of Nations*
Nassim Nicholas Taleb's *The Black Swan: The Impact of the Highly Improbable*
Amos Tversky's & Daniel Kahneman's *Judgment under Uncertainty: Heuristics and Biases*
Mahbub Ul Haq's *Reflections on Human Development*
Max Weber's *The Protestant Ethic and the Spirit of Capitalism*

FEMINISM AND GENDER STUDIES

Judith Butler's *Gender Trouble*
Simone De Beauvoir's *The Second Sex*
Michel Foucault's *History of Sexuality*
Betty Friedan's *The Feminine Mystique*
Saba Mahmood's *The Politics of Piety: The Islamic Revival and the Feminist Subject*
Joan Wallach Scott's *Gender and the Politics of History*
Mary Wollstonecraft's *A Vindication of the Rights of Woman*
Virginia Woolf's *A Room of One's Own*

GEOGRAPHY

The Brundtland Report's *Our Common Future*
Rachel Carson's *Silent Spring*
Charles Darwin's *On the Origin of Species*
James Ferguson's *The Anti-Politics Machine*
Jane Jacobs's *The Death and Life of Great American Cities*
James Lovelock's *Gaia: A New Look at Life on Earth*
Amartya Sen's *Development as Freedom*
Mathis Wackernagel & William Rees's *Our Ecological Footprint*

HISTORY

Janet Abu-Lughod's *Before European Hegemony*
Benedict Anderson's *Imagined Communities*
Bernard Bailyn's *The Ideological Origins of the American Revolution*
Hanna Batatu's *The Old Social Classes And The Revolutionary Movements Of Iraq*
Christopher Browning's *Ordinary Men: Reserve Police Batallion 101 and the Final Solution in Poland*
Edmund Burke's *Reflections on the Revolution in France*
William Cronon's *Nature's Metropolis: Chicago And The Great West*
Alfred W. Crosby's *The Columbian Exchange*
Hamid Dabashi's *Iran: A People Interrupted*
David Brion Davis's *The Problem of Slavery in the Age of Revolution*
Nathalie Zemon Davis's *The Return of Martin Guerre*
Jared Diamond's *Guns, Germs & Steel: the Fate of Human Societies*
Frank Dikotter's *Mao's Great Famine*
John W Dower's *War Without Mercy: Race And Power In The Pacific War*
W. E. B. Du Bois's *The Souls of Black Folk*
Richard J. Evans's *In Defence of History*
Lucien Febvre's *The Problem of Unbelief in the 16th Century*
Sheila Fitzpatrick's *Everyday Stalinism*

The Macat Library By Discipline

Eric Foner's *Reconstruction: America's Unfinished Revolution, 1863-1877*
Michel Foucault's *Discipline and Punish*
Michel Foucault's *History of Sexuality*
Francis Fukuyama's *The End of History and the Last Man*
John Lewis Gaddis's *We Now Know: Rethinking Cold War History*
Ernest Gellner's *Nations and Nationalism*
Eugene Genovese's *Roll, Jordan, Roll: The World the Slaves Made*
Carlo Ginzburg's *The Night Battles*
Daniel Goldhagen's *Hitler's Willing Executioners*
Jack Goldstone's *Revolution and Rebellion in the Early Modern World*
Antonio Gramsci's *The Prison Notebooks*
Alexander Hamilton, John Jay & James Madison's *The Federalist Papers*
Christopher Hill's *The World Turned Upside Down*
Carole Hillenbrand's *The Crusades: Islamic Perspectives*
Thomas Hobbes's *Leviathan*
Eric Hobsbawm's *The Age Of Revolution*
John A. Hobson's *Imperialism: A Study*
Albert Hourani's *History of the Arab Peoples*
Samuel P. Huntington's *The Clash of Civilizations and the Remaking of World Order*
C. L. R. James's *The Black Jacobins*
Tony Judt's *Postwar: A History of Europe Since 1945*
Ernst Kantorowicz's *The King's Two Bodies: A Study in Medieval Political Theology*
Paul Kennedy's *The Rise and Fall of the Great Powers*
Ian Kershaw's *The "Hitler Myth": Image and Reality in the Third Reich*
John Maynard Keynes's *The General Theory of Employment, Interest and Money*
Charles P. Kindleberger's *Manias, Panics and Crashes*
Martin Luther King Jr's *Why We Can't Wait*
Henry Kissinger's *World Order: Reflections on the Character of Nations and the Course of History*
Thomas Kuhn's *The Structure of Scientific Revolutions*
Georges Lefebvre's *The Coming of the French Revolution*
John Locke's *Two Treatises of Government*
Niccolò Machiavelli's *The Prince*
Thomas Robert Malthus's *An Essay on the Principle of Population*
Mahmood Mamdani's *Citizen and Subject: Contemporary Africa And The Legacy Of Late Colonialism*
Karl Marx's *Capital*
Stanley Milgram's *Obedience to Authority*
John Stuart Mill's *On Liberty*
Thomas Paine's *Common Sense*
Thomas Paine's *Rights of Man*
Geoffrey Parker's *Global Crisis: War, Climate Change and Catastrophe in the Seventeenth Century*
Jonathan Riley-Smith's *The First Crusade and the Idea of Crusading*
Jean-Jacques Rousseau's *The Social Contract*
Joan Wallach Scott's *Gender and the Politics of History*
Theda Skocpol's *States and Social Revolutions*
Adam Smith's *The Wealth of Nations*
Timothy Snyder's *Bloodlands: Europe Between Hitler and Stalin*
Sun Tzu's *The Art of War*
Keith Thomas's *Religion and the Decline of Magic*
Thucydides's *The History of the Peloponnesian War*
Frederick Jackson Turner's *The Significance of the Frontier in American History*
Odd Arne Westad's *The Global Cold War: Third World Interventions And The Making Of Our Times*

LITERATURE

Chinua Achebe's *An Image of Africa: Racism in Conrad's Heart of Darkness*
Roland Barthes's *Mythologies*
Homi K. Bhabha's *The Location of Culture*
Judith Butler's *Gender Trouble*
Simone De Beauvoir's *The Second Sex*
Ferdinand De Saussure's *Course in General Linguistics*
T. S. Eliot's *The Sacred Wood: Essays on Poetry and Criticism*
Zora Neale Huston's *Characteristics of Negro Expression*
Toni Morrison's *Playing in the Dark: Whiteness in the American Literary Imagination*
Edward Said's *Orientalism*
Gayatri Chakravorty Spivak's *Can the Subaltern Speak?*
Mary Wollstonecraft's *A Vindication of the Rights of Women*
Virginia Woolf's *A Room of One's Own*

PHILOSOPHY

Elizabeth Anscombe's *Modern Moral Philosophy*
Hannah Arendt's *The Human Condition*
Aristotle's *Metaphysics*
Aristotle's *Nicomachean Ethics*
Edmund Gettier's *Is Justified True Belief Knowledge?*
Georg Wilhelm Friedrich Hegel's *Phenomenology of Spirit*
David Hume's *Dialogues Concerning Natural Religion*
David Hume's *The Enquiry for Human Understanding*
Immanuel Kant's *Religion within the Boundaries of Mere Reason*
Immanuel Kant's *Critique of Pure Reason*
Søren Kierkegaard's *The Sickness Unto Death*
Søren Kierkegaard's *Fear and Trembling*
C. S. Lewis's *The Abolition of Man*
Alasdair MacIntyre's *After Virtue*
Marcus Aurelius's *Meditations*
Friedrich Nietzsche's *On the Genealogy of Morality*
Friedrich Nietzsche's *Beyond Good and Evil*
Plato's *Republic*
Plato's *Symposium*
Jean-Jacques Rousseau's *The Social Contract*
Gilbert Ryle's *The Concept of Mind*
Baruch Spinoza's *Ethics*
Sun Tzu's *The Art of War*
Ludwig Wittgenstein's *Philosophical Investigations*

POLITICS

Benedict Anderson's *Imagined Communities*
Aristotle's *Politics*
Bernard Bailyn's *The Ideological Origins of the American Revolution*
Edmund Burke's *Reflections on the Revolution in France*
John C. Calhoun's *A Disquisition on Government*
Ha-Joon Chang's *Kicking Away the Ladder*
Hamid Dabashi's *Iran: A People Interrupted*
Hamid Dabashi's *Theology of Discontent: The Ideological Foundation of the Islamic Revolution in Iran*
Robert Dahl's *Democracy and its Critics*
Robert Dahl's *Who Governs?*
David Brion Davis's *The Problem of Slavery in the Age of Revolution*

The Macat Library By Discipline

Alexis De Tocqueville's *Democracy in America*
James Ferguson's *The Anti-Politics Machine*
Frank Dikotter's *Mao's Great Famine*
Sheila Fitzpatrick's *Everyday Stalinism*
Eric Foner's *Reconstruction: America's Unfinished Revolution, 1863-1877*
Milton Friedman's *Capitalism and Freedom*
Francis Fukuyama's *The End of History and the Last Man*
John Lewis Gaddis's *We Now Know: Rethinking Cold War History*
Ernest Gellner's *Nations and Nationalism*
David Graeber's *Debt: the First 5000 Years*
Antonio Gramsci's *The Prison Notebooks*
Alexander Hamilton, John Jay & James Madison's *The Federalist Papers*
Friedrich Hayek's *The Road to Serfdom*
Christopher Hill's *The World Turned Upside Down*
Thomas Hobbes's *Leviathan*
John A. Hobson's *Imperialism: A Study*
Samuel P. Huntington's *The Clash of Civilizations and the Remaking of World Order*
Tony Judt's *Postwar: A History of Europe Since 1945*
David C. Kang's *China Rising: Peace, Power and Order in East Asia*
Paul Kennedy's *The Rise and Fall of Great Powers*
Robert Keohane's *After Hegemony*
Martin Luther King Jr.'s *Why We Can't Wait*
Henry Kissinger's *World Order: Reflections on the Character of Nations and the Course of History*
John Locke's *Two Treatises of Government*
Niccolò Machiavelli's *The Prince*
Thomas Robert Malthus's *An Essay on the Principle of Population*
Mahmood Mamdani's *Citizen and Subject: Contemporary Africa And The Legacy Of Late Colonialism*
Karl Marx's *Capital*
John Stuart Mill's *On Liberty*
John Stuart Mill's *Utilitarianism*
Hans Morgenthau's *Politics Among Nations*
Thomas Paine's *Common Sense*
Thomas Paine's *Rights of Man*
Thomas Piketty's *Capital in the Twenty-First Century*
Robert D. Putman's *Bowling Alone*
John Rawls's *Theory of Justice*
Jean-Jacques Rousseau's *The Social Contract*
Theda Skocpol's *States and Social Revolutions*
Adam Smith's *The Wealth of Nations*
Sun Tzu's *The Art of War*
Henry David Thoreau's *Civil Disobedience*
Thucydides's *The History of the Peloponnesian War*
Kenneth Waltz's *Theory of International Politics*
Max Weber's *Politics as a Vocation*
Odd Arne Westad's *The Global Cold War: Third World Interventions And The Making Of Our Times*

POSTCOLONIAL STUDIES

Roland Barthes's *Mythologies*
Frantz Fanon's *Black Skin, White Masks*
Homi K. Bhabha's *The Location of Culture*
Gustavo Gutiérrez's *A Theology of Liberation*
Edward Said's *Orientalism*
Gayatri Chakravorty Spivak's *Can the Subaltern Speak?*

PSYCHOLOGY

Gordon Allport's *The Nature of Prejudice*
Alan Baddeley & Graham Hitch's *Aggression: A Social Learning Analysis*
Albert Bandura's *Aggression: A Social Learning Analysis*
Leon Festinger's *A Theory of Cognitive Dissonance*
Sigmund Freud's *The Interpretation of Dreams*
Betty Friedan's *The Feminine Mystique*
Michael R. Gottfredson & Travis Hirschi's *A General Theory of Crime*
Eric Hoffer's *The True Believer: Thoughts on the Nature of Mass Movements*
William James's *Principles of Psychology*
Elizabeth Loftus's *Eyewitness Testimony*
A. H. Maslow's *A Theory of Human Motivation*
Stanley Milgram's *Obedience to Authority*
Steven Pinker's *The Better Angels of Our Nature*
Oliver Sacks's *The Man Who Mistook His Wife For a Hat*
Richard Thaler & Cass Sunstein's *Nudge: Improving Decisions About Health, Wealth and Happiness*
Amos Tversky's *Judgment under Uncertainty: Heuristics and Biases*
Philip Zimbardo's *The Lucifer Effect*

SCIENCE

Rachel Carson's *Silent Spring*
William Cronon's *Nature's Metropolis: Chicago And The Great West*
Alfred W. Crosby's *The Columbian Exchange*
Charles Darwin's *On the Origin of Species*
Richard Dawkin's *The Selfish Gene*
Thomas Kuhn's *The Structure of Scientific Revolutions*
Geoffrey Parker's *Global Crisis: War, Climate Change and Catastrophe in the Seventeenth Century*
Mathis Wackernagel & William Rees's *Our Ecological Footprint*

SOCIOLOGY

Michelle Alexander's *The New Jim Crow: Mass Incarceration in the Age of Colorblindness*
Gordon Allport's *The Nature of Prejudice*
Albert Bandura's *Aggression: A Social Learning Analysis*
Hanna Batatu's *The Old Social Classes And The Revolutionary Movements Of Iraq*
Ha-Joon Chang's *Kicking Away the Ladder*
W. E. B. Du Bois's *The Souls of Black Folk*
Émile Durkheim's *On Suicide*
Frantz Fanon's *Black Skin, White Masks*
Frantz Fanon's *The Wretched of the Earth*
Eric Foner's *Reconstruction: America's Unfinished Revolution, 1863-1877*
Eugene Genovese's *Roll, Jordan, Roll: The World the Slaves Made*
Jack Goldstone's *Revolution and Rebellion in the Early Modern World*
Antonio Gramsci's *The Prison Notebooks*
Richard Herrnstein & Charles A Murray's *The Bell Curve: Intelligence and Class Structure in American Life*
Eric Hoffer's *The True Believer: Thoughts on the Nature of Mass Movements*
Jane Jacobs's *The Death and Life of Great American Cities*
Robert Lucas's *Why Doesn't Capital Flow from Rich to Poor Countries?*
Jay Macleod's *Ain't No Makin' It: Aspirations and Attainment in a Low Income Neighborhood*
Elaine May's *Homeward Bound: American Families in the Cold War Era*
Douglas McGregor's *The Human Side of Enterprise*
C. Wright Mills's *The Sociological Imagination*

The Macat Library By Discipline

Thomas Piketty's *Capital in the Twenty-First Century*
Robert D. Putman's *Bowling Alone*
David Riesman's *The Lonely Crowd: A Study of the Changing American Character*
Edward Said's *Orientalism*
Joan Wallach Scott's *Gender and the Politics of History*
Theda Skocpol's *States and Social Revolutions*
Max Weber's *The Protestant Ethic and the Spirit of Capitalism*

THEOLOGY

Augustine's *Confessions*
Benedict's *Rule of St Benedict*
Gustavo Gutiérrez's *A Theology of Liberation*
Carole Hillenbrand's *The Crusades: Islamic Perspectives*
David Hume's *Dialogues Concerning Natural Religion*
Immanuel Kant's *Religion within the Boundaries of Mere Reason*
Ernst Kantorowicz's *The King's Two Bodies: A Study in Medieval Political Theology*
Søren Kierkegaard's *The Sickness Unto Death*
C. S. Lewis's *The Abolition of Man*
Saba Mahmood's *The Politics of Piety: The Islamic Revival and the Feminist Subject*
Baruch Spinoza's *Ethics*
Keith Thomas's *Religion and the Decline of Magic*

COMING SOON

Chris Argyris's *The Individual and the Organisation*
Seyla Benhabib's *The Rights of Others*
Walter Benjamin's *The Work Of Art in the Age of Mechanical Reproduction*
John Berger's *Ways of Seeing*
Pierre Bourdieu's *Outline of a Theory of Practice*
Mary Douglas's *Purity and Danger*
Roland Dworkin's *Taking Rights Seriously*
James G. March's *Exploration and Exploitation in Organisational Learning*
Ikujiro Nonaka's *A Dynamic Theory of Organizational Knowledge Creation*
Griselda Pollock's *Vision and Difference*
Amartya Sen's *Inequality Re-Examined*
Susan Sontag's *On Photography*
Yasser Tabbaa's *The Transformation of Islamic Art*
Ludwig von Mises's *Theory of Money and Credit*

Macat Disciplines

Access the greatest ideas and thinkers across entire disciplines, including

Postcolonial Studies

Roland Barthes's *Mythologies*
Frantz Fanon's *Black Skin, White Masks*
Homi K. Bhabha's *The Location of Culture*
Gustavo Gutiérrez's *A Theology of Liberation*
Edward Said's *Orientalism*
Gayatri Chakravorty Spivak's *Can the Subaltern Speak?*

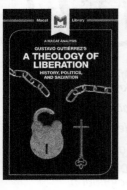
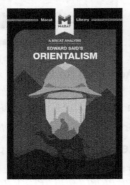

Macat Disciplines

Access the greatest ideas and thinkers across entire disciplines, including

AFRICANA STUDIES

Chinua Achebe's *An Image of Africa: Racism in Conrad's Heart of Darkness*

W. E. B. Du Bois's *The Souls of Black Folk*

Zora Neale Hurston's *Characteristics of Negro Expression*

Martin Luther King Jr.'s *Why We Can't Wait*

Toni Morrison's *Playing in the Dark: Whiteness in the American Literary Imagination*

Macat Disciplines

Access the greatest ideas and thinkers across entire disciplines, including

FEMINISM, GENDER AND QUEER STUDIES

Simone De Beauvoir's
The Second Sex

Michel Foucault's
History of Sexuality

Betty Friedan's
The Feminine Mystique

Saba Mahmood's
*The Politics of Piety:
The Islamic Revival and
the Feminist Subject*

Joan Wallach Scott's
*Gender and the
Politics of History*

Mary Wollstonecraft's
*A Vindication of the
Rights of Woman*

Virginia Woolf's
A Room of One's Own

Judith Butler's
Gender Trouble

 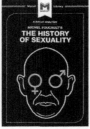